DIVORCE
legal procedures and financial facts

a Consumer Publication

edited by Edith Rudinger

published by Consumers' Association
publishers of **Which?**

Consumer publications
are available from
Consumers' Association
and from booksellers.

© Consumers' Association July 1984

ISBN 0 85202 275 1
and 0 340 35248 5

 Printed in Great Britain by
Page Bros (Norwich) Ltd

DIVORCE
legal procedures
and financial facts

a Consumer Publication

Consumers' Association
publishers of **Which?**
14 Buckingham Street
London WC2N 6DS

Contents

Changes in the law

At the time of this book going to press (June 1984), the Matrimonial and Family Proceedings Bill was at the final stages of going through parliament; it received royal assent on 12 July 1984.

Some of the provisions of the new Act due to come into force on 12 October 1984 which affect what is in this book include

* the length of time a marriage has been in existence before a divorce petition can be filed (*pages 12, 210*)
* the criteria for assessing maintenance and other financial or property adjustment (*page 92 et seq*)
* the consideration of 'conduct' when deciding on maintenance (*pages 92, 97, 98*)
* the duration of maintenance orders where there are no children (*pages 67, 92, 180*)
* consent to the dismissal of a claim for financial provision (*pages 67, 128*).

Divorce and your pocket

Divorce has only relatively recently become easy to obtain, and many people still see the divorce decree as the main hurdle. It is not – the major problems are nearly always about money, housing and children.

People may try to protect themselves against the effects of events such as redundancy, serious illness, disabling accident, death of husband or wife – by taking out life or accident insurance, for example. If and when divorce comes, not only will you not have made any provision for it but you may not even expect it to be the financial disaster that it can turn out to be. You may have to cope with many intense emotions: perhaps a sense of failure, loneliness and depression, feelings of resentment or hatred towards your partner and distress over the children. While all this is going on, it may not be easy to think sensibly about financial arrangements, apart from the short-term provision of everyday needs for yourself and your children – getting through the next day is often as much as you can cope with. Alternatively, you may find yourself on a temporary 'high' from feelings of release and the prospect of a new beginning.

It may be months or even years before your emotions settle down, indeed they may never do so, but one thing is certain – your life and the way you live is bound to change.

spending rush

Faced with a broken marriage, it is not uncommon for life to seem unreal and one of the ways in which this sometimes comes out is a change in your spending pattern (assuming the money is there – and often even if it is not).

You may find yourself wanting to blow money on redecorating the house and buying new equipment. You may go out more often to avoid being alone or try and start new relationships. If you sit it out at home, staying up until the early hours of the morning talking on the telephone to friends, you may find that the heating and lighting and 'phone bills go up; you may start spending more money on cigarettes and alcohol. Both women and men may feel that they have to have their hair done more often and better, or buy uncharacteristically expensive clothes, because they think they have been rejected for their 'looks'.

If the change in your spending pattern is not recognised, money may be frittered away, and any capital you had managed to accumulate will soon have gone so that there will no longer be any reserve for unexpected bills or expenses.

standard of living

Whatever your standard of living was before the divorce, you have to accept that it is going to drop, often quite drastically, especially where you have children and/or only one of you is working.

In some cases, money is so limited that it would be quite pointless arguing for months, either privately or with the assistance of solicitors: unless the money facts change, there is nothing that can be done. The problem nearly always comes down to the fact that two homes have to be found and run, rather than one.

Be realistic: do not expect that somehow there will be more money than there was before. Unless some good fortune comes your way, neither of you will be able to change the inevitable financial result very much, if at all, and the sooner you come to terms with this, the better for everybody.

Although you and your partner are divorcing because the marriage relationship between the two of you has come to an end, you should still be able to trust each other as rational, intelligent people – at least enough to make proper arrangements for your children's future and your own.

Like it or not, realities have to be faced and the sooner you and your husband or wife get down to sorting out your financial affairs the better.

ways in which divorce will hit your pocket

Not all of the ways in which people suffer financially on divorce will apply to your situation. For example, if you are both in your late twenties, have no children and both have good jobs and have been buying a house together on mortgage for the last few years, it may be that you can split up without it costing either of you too much. On the other hand, if you have small children, or one of you is unemployed, or has not worked for many years, you are both going to suffer, because there will now be two households and only one income to support them.

two homes to run and furnish

As well as the rent or mortgage on the matrimonial home and the standard bills for rates, water charges, gas and electricity to be paid, the money for similar charges will now have to be found for the new home by or for the person who is moving out.

The loss of the status of owner-occupier, usually by the man, is often the root cause of more resentment than any other factor, particularly where he does not regard himself in any way to blame for the breakdown.

Generally, whoever is moving out will suffer, at least temporarily, a substantial reduction in the quality of his or her home environment.

Quite apart from the running costs, even if you agree to split the contents of your existing home, there may still be the cost of buying some duplicate furniture and household equipment – another cooker, refrigerator and possibly a washing machine – unless one of you is moving into an already furnished flat, or lodgings.

The person who remains may well find that he or she does not have sufficient money to run the house in the same way as before, and gas, electricity and other bills which at one time were paid without a thought, are now awaited with dread.

If you are the spouse left behind in the home, you should not assume that you will be able to afford to stay there, even if you can get maintenance or some other financial support. One side-effect of the break-up of the marriage may be that you lose your job or have to give it up. If there is a large mortgage financed by the job, it is better to be realistic sooner rather than later.

costs of moving

If whoever is moving out is buying a home, there may be some or all of

★ conveyancing fees
★ building society's solicitor's fees
★ surveyor's fees
★ mortgage broker's fees (you may need help to find a mortgage on a second home)
★ stamp duty if the purchase price is over £30,000.

If you are selling your old home, splitting the proceeds and both buying new homes, you will probably have to pay

★ three sets of conveyancing fees: one sale and two purchases
★ two sets of surveyor's valuation fees (if you are both going to take out new mortgages) and structural survey fees
★ bridging finance on one or both properties
★ two items of stamp duty if the price of the house(s) is over £30,000
★ estate agent's commission on the sale of your old home
★ two sets of mortgagee's solicitors' fees
★ two sets of removal charges (even if only one of you is moving out and going into rented accommodation, there may be removal expenses).

If there is no suitable accommodation in the area (either because buying is too expensive or there is no rented accommodation available), this may involve increased travelling costs to work for whoever has moved out.

changed costs of living

Unless you are a two-car family, one of you is going to lose the use of what was the family car. Not only may this involve additional expense in using public transport, but it can also be considerably inconvenient – for example, if you used the car to run the children to school.

Food is not such a substantial item as accommodation, but it may nevertheless cause additional expense. A man now living on his own, for example, not used to cooking for himself, may feed himself uneconomically by eating out, or buying prepared convenience foods.

During the course of your marriage, both of you will have done many unpaid tasks around the house which you may not now have time or ability to do for yourself. For example, you may have to employ somebody to do the cleaning, washing and ironing, or pay someone to do various do-it-yourself jobs around the house.

For the parent who has moved out, seeing the children may involve substantial travelling costs (for them to visit you or you to go to them) and extra expense on outings, especially if it is not practical to have them to stay. The one who has moved out may also feel a need, especially in the early stages, to buy the children extra, compensatory, treats.

Generally speaking, you will find that in financial terms, you have lost more than you have gained. But this may be more than made up for by release from a relationship that has become an intolerable burden to one or both of you.

Getting a divorce

The sole ground for a divorce in England or Wales is the irretrievable breakdown of the marriage. A marriage is not held to have broken down irretrievably unless the petitioner satisfies the divorce court of one or more of the following facts

1 that the respondent has committed adultery and the petitioner finds it intolerable to live with the respondent

2 that the respondent has behaved in such a way that the petitioner cannot reasonably be expected to live with the respondent

3 that the respondent has deserted the petitioner for a continuous period of at least two years immediately preceding the presentation of the petition

4 that the parties have lived apart for a continuous period of at least two years immediately preceding the presentation of the petition and that the respondent consents to a decree being granted

5 that the parties have lived apart for a continuous period of at least five years immediately preceding the presentation of the petition.

Divorce cannot be petitioned for until three years after the marriage took place and will not be granted unless satisfactory arrangements have been made for the children of the family. (When the Matrimonial and Family Proceedings Bill comes into force (probably in the autumn of 1984), it will be possible to petition for divorce after one year of marriage.)

The husband or the wife must be domiciled in England or Wales or have been resident there for at least one year before the date of presenting the petition. Short absences, for example for holidays, can be ignored.

It is advisable to consult a solicitor straightaway in connection with any proposed divorce where there is doubt about domicile or when neither of the couple lives in England or Wales.

Domicile or residence in Scotland, Northern Ireland, the Channel Islands, the Isle of Man is not sufficient to enable a person to petition for divorce in an english court.

judicial separation

A petition for judicial separation can be presented at any time after marriage and makes it possible for a spouse to get a court order for financial or property provision. The effect of a decree is that the petitioner is no longer under any legal obligation to reside with the respondent but, in law, the couple remain married, so neither can marry anyone else. A decree of judicial separation does not preclude a divorce later and it would then not be necessary to produce further evidence of the marriage having broken down.

The procedure for obtaining a decree of judicial separation is similar to divorce but there is only one decree, with no interim stage.

the procedure

Whichever of a couple formally initiates the divorce is called the petitioner, the other spouse is the respondent.

In an undefended case, a solicitor is not needed for the actual procedure of getting divorced. However, you may want advice from a solicitor before embarking on divorce proceedings. You may want to check whether there are grounds for divorce in your case and that you understand what has to be done, by whom and when, and what the implications are of the questions you will be required to answer on the various forms that have to be completed and submitted to the court.

In an undefended divorce by the special procedure system, there is normally no hearing in open court. The facts in the petition (and subsequent affidavits) are considered by the registrar of the divorce court without either spouse being present.

documents needed

To start divorce proceedings, the following will be needed

- the completed form of petition for divorce, with a copy for the other spouse (the respondent) plus an extra copy in an adultery case where the co-respondent is named
- the marriage certificate (or a certified copy).

A photocopy of the marriage certificate is not acceptable. A certified copy can be obtained, for a fee, from the General Register Office, St Catherines House, 10 Kingsway, London WC2B 6JP, or from the superintendent registrar of births, deaths and marriages for the district or the incumbent of the church where the marriage took place (the marriage certificate will not be returned to you)

- a fee of £40 (or a completed fee-exemption form if you are exempted because you are receiving supplementary benefit or family income supplement, or legal advice under the green form scheme)

- a statement of the proposed arrangements for any relevant children, with a copy for the other spouse.

Whichever spouse is the petitioner sends or takes the papers to any divorce county court or to the Divorce Registry in London (Somerset House, Strand, London WC2R 1LP). Not all county courts deal with divorces; check with your local one (listed under 'courts' in the telephone directory).

Forms for the petition and for the statement of arrangements for children are available from divorce court offices and the Divorce Registry, without charge, and also a free booklet *Undefended divorce – a guide for the petitioner acting without a solicitor*.

You should keep a copy for yourself of any document that you supply to the court or to the other spouse.

A reference number will be allocated to your petition by the court and must be quoted on all communications to the court throughout the case.

the petition

There is a standard printed form of petition for each of the five facts, obtainable from the divorce court office. With the form of petition, the court supplies notes for guidance which you should read carefully before completing your petition.

In some courts, the staff will help you complete the forms but they are not allowed to give you legal advice.

In the petition, you must give the date of the marriage, the address at which you and your spouse last lived together and your present address(es); the occupations of yourself and spouse; the names and dates of birth of children; details of any previous court proceedings relating to the marriage or property.

You must set out one or more of the five facts on which you rely to show that the marriage has irretrievably broken down. Eventually you will have to give evidence of the facts, normally by affidavit (a sworn statement).

fact 1 **adultery and intolerability**

In the petition, no more need be said than that the respondent has committed adultery with the co-respondent (whose identity or name and address should be given, if known). It is useful but not necessary to say when and where adultery has taken place. In addition, the petitioner must state that he or she finds it intolerable to live with the other spouse.

(A petitioner in Northern Ireland has to prove the respondent's adultery only and not that he or she also finds it intolerable to live with the respondent.)

fact 2 **unreasonable behaviour**

There is no simple definition of unreasonable behaviour. The law says 'that the respondent has behaved in such a way that the petitioner cannot reasonably be expected to live with the respondent'. Violence or serious threats of violence to the petitioner or to the children, homosexual conduct, persistent nagging, refusal to have sexual intercourse or to have children knowing that the other spouse wished to have them, insistence on abortion against the wishes of the other, financial irresponsibility such as gambling to excess, other persistent extravagance to the detriment of the family's welfare – are some examples of what can amount to unreasonable behaviour. Even behaviour caused by insanity is taken into account, but many less grave matters are sufficient.

The test is whether the court feels that between the particular husband and wife the behaviour complained of is sufficiently serious to make it unreasonable to expect the petitioner to go on living with the respondent. A single serious incident might be sufficient, but usually there will have to have been a number of incidents, and the longer the conduct complained of has been going on, the more likely is it for behaviour that would be relatively trivial in isolation to be regarded as sufficient to justify divorce.

If the behaviour of one of the spouses has forced the other to leave home, this would be evidence of the unreasonableness of the behaviour.

In the petition, you should set out a fairly precise account of the alleged behaviour, giving details, with the approximate dates and places preferably in date order, of incidents of importance that led to the breakdown of the marriage, so that the respondent can know what is alleged and the registrar can decide whether the behaviour was unreasonable.

Where you have continued to live together, it is particularly important that details of incidents of unreasonable behaviour within the last six months are included in the petition. Further evidence can, if necessary, be given in the affidavit that follows the petition.

fact 3 **desertion**
Desertion as the basis for divorce means a period of separation of at least two years brought about by husband or wife leaving the other against the other one's wishes. You have to state the circumstances, the date when he or she left, and that it was without your consent.

facts 4 and 5 **separation**
In order to establish separation as proof of the breakdown of a marriage, a couple must have lived apart for at least two years if the respondent consents to the divorce, or for more than five years if there is no consent. The date of separation should be stated in the petition as accurately as possible.

If the separation has been for more than two but less than five years, the respondent's positive consent to being divorced is necessary – not just lack of objection.

After five or more years' separation, the respondent's consent is not required (but there is provision for opposing on the grounds of grave financial or other hardship). The respondent's financial position as a result of being divorced will be closely scrutinised and the petitioner may have to provide more generously for the respondent in order to obtain a decree.

In all separation cases, the respondent may request that his or her future financial position be considered by the court before the decree is made final.

six months for attempted reconciliation

On the affidavit that has to follow the petition, there are questions about relevant dates of living in the same household. To allow for attempts at reconciliation, the couple can have gone on living together for a period of up to six months, or several shorter periods adding up to not more than six months.

adultery

Where a petitioner became aware of the other's adultery, a period of living together which has exceeded six months by the time the decree nisi stage has been reached (or even the stage of applying for the decree to be made absolute) would prevent a decree, even though the period may have been less than six months at the date of the petition.

unreasonable behaviour

Where unreasonable behaviour is alleged in the petition, the six months of living together are counted from the last act of unreasonable behaviour and are taken into account in deciding whether the petitioner can reasonably be expected to live with the respondent.

Living together for more than six months would not necessarily prevent a decree being granted, but the court would require a detailed explanation and may well conclude that the respondent's behaviour was not unreasonable.

separation

Although periods of living together totalling not more than six months since separation or desertion will not invalidate the divorce petition, any such period will not count as part of the two years or five years. For instance, if the couple has lived together for three months in an attempt at reconciliation (which has failed) and then parted again, the petition cannot be filed until two years and three months have elapsed since the original separation.

Before completing this form, read carefully the attached *NOTES FOR GUIDANCE*

IN THE   COUNTY COURT*   * Delete as
                                                                  appropriate

IN THE DIVORCE REGISTRY*   No.

(1) On the   day of   19   the petitioner
                                                   was lawfully married to
                                                   (hereinafter called "the
respondent") at

(2) The petitioner and respondent last lived together at

(3) The petitioner is domiciled in England and Wales, and is by occupation a
                              and resides at
                                                       and the respondent
is by occupation a
                              and resides at

(4) There are no children of the family now living *except*

(5) No other child, now living, has been born to the petitioner/respondent during the marriage
(so far as is known to the petitioner) *except*

D.8.

Dd 8304023 300M 8/82 Ed(202073)

(6) There are or have been no other proceedings in any court in England and Wales or elsewhere with reference to the marriage (or to any child of the family) or between the petitioner and respondent with reference to any property of either or both of them *except*

(7) There are no proceedings continuing in any country outside England or Wales which are in respect of the marriage or are capable of affecting its validity or subsistence *except*

(8) (This paragraph should be completed only if the petition is based on five years' separation.) No agreement or arrangement has been made or is proposed to be made between the parties for the support of the petitioner/respondent (and any child of the family) *except*

(9) The said marriage has broken down irretrievably.

(10)

The 'prayer'

The last page of the petition contains the petitioner's formal request (prayer) that the marriage be dissolved.

This is the place for the petitioner also to ask for custody of children; for the costs of the case to be paid by the other side; and, under the heading of 'ancillary relief', for orders for maintenance (called periodical payments), lump sum payments and property adjustment.

It is better, at this stage, not to cross anything off the list of requests, because it may be complicated or even impossible to apply later, but do not specify any actual amounts at this stage.

If the requests are not left standing in the prayer, the petitioner would have to make a special application to the court for leave to apply later for any required order. Such an application is not certain to be granted if it is made after a long time lag or if, for example, the respondent said that he or she decided not to defend the petition only because of the absence of any request for ancillary relief.

If you have agreed with your spouse that all financial claims (or some claims) are to be dismissed, then put in the prayer 'for dismissal purposes only', to avoid misunderstanding and distress when your spouse receives the petition.

statement as to arrangements for children

All children of the family, whatever their age, have to be named in the petition. 'Children of the family' are, in broad terms, children who are children of both husband and wife, children adopted by them both, step-children, and other children who have been treated at any time during the marriage by both as part of the family – but not foster-children.

A statement about the proposed arrangements for relevant children must be signed by the petitioner and sent (plus copy for other spouse) with the petition. (A printed form for this statement is available from the court office.) Relevant children are those under the age of 16, or under the age of 18 and receiving instruction at an educational establishment or undergoing training for a trade, profession or vocation (even if the child is also earning). If a child over 16 and under 18 is not still being educated or trained, it is useful to say so in the petition.

PRAYER

The petitioner therefore prays:—

(1)   That the said marriage be dissolved.

(2)   That the petitioner may be granted the custody of

(3)   That the   may be ordered to pay the costs of this suit.

(4)   That the petitioner may be granted the following ancillary relief:
    (a)   an order for maintenance pending suit
        a periodical payments order
        a secured provision order
        a lump sum order

    (b)   a periodical payments order
        a secured provision order   } for the children of the family
        a lump sum order

    (c)   a property adjustment order

Signed

The names and addresses of the persons to be served with this petition are:—

Respondent:—

Co-Respondent (adultery case only):—

The Petitioner's address for service is:—

Dated this   day of   19

Address all communications for the court to: The Chief Clerk, County Court,

The Court
office at

is open from 10 a.m. to 4 p.m. (4.30 p.m. at the Divorce Registry) on Mondays to Fridays.

Among the particulars to be given in the statement is information about where each child is to live, including details of the accommodation, names of other persons living there and who will look after the children. Details of financial provisions have to be given, stating who is at present supporting the children, and whether an application will be made to the court for their financial support.

The name of the school or other educational establishment which each child does or will attend has to be given or, if he is working, his place of employment, the nature of his work and of any training he will receive.

The respondent

The court sends to the respondent, at the address given in the petition, one copy of the petition and, where appropriate, of the statement as to the arrangements for children.

The court also sends an 'acknowledgment of service' form, which the respondent should complete and return to the court within 8 days. (If adultery is alleged and a co-respondent is named, a copy of the petition is sent to him or her, also with an acknowledgment of service form to be returned to the court.) With the documents is sent an explanatory leaflet called 'notice of proceedings'.

The acknowledgment of service is not only an acknowledgment that the petition has been received; it includes questions about the respondent's intentions, such as whether he or she wishes to defend, wishes to be heard on the matter of costs or custody, or wishes to make an application for custody or access on his or her own behalf.

In an adultery case, the respondent is asked to indicate if he or she admits adultery and to sign the acknowledgment of service even if a solicitor is also signing.

In a separation case, the respondent has to reply to the question on the acknowledgment of service form whether he or she intends to apply for the court to consider the financial position as it will be after the divorce.

Where it is a separation with consent, the respondent has to confirm consent by saying 'yes' and also putting his or her signature on the form. (Consent may be withdrawn, by writing to the court, at any time before the decree nisi is pronounced.)

If the respondent does not agree to the proposed arrangements about children, he or she should send to the court two copies of a signed statement containing counter-proposals. This can best be done by using the standard form of statement as to arrangements, although a statement in any other form would be acceptable.

All financial matters and arrangements for children are dealt with as separate issues, irrespective of whether the divorce itself is defended or undefended.

defending

If the respondent does not agree to the divorce, he or she has to file an 'answer' to the petition denying the allegations. (Preparing an answer should be done with the help of a solicitor.) It is important that the respondent files an answer promptly. If he or she neglects to do so, he or she may find that the registrar has given a certificate for the decree nisi on the basis of the petition and it will be too late to file an answer (except with special leave of the court).

After an answer has been filed, the registrar fixes an appointment in his chambers when both parties (with their solicitors if they are represented) will be required to attend. The registrar will see if there is any way of avoiding a defended divorce. He may ask the parties to see a divorce court welfare officer to discuss the possibilities of reaching a compromise. Only if these efforts fail will the registrar allow the cause to go forward to a hearing.

The hearing will be in open court before a High Court judge in London or one of the major provincial court centres. A defended divorce would need a solicitor on each side and may also need the services of barristers when it gets to court.

If, however, the respondent files an answer not denying the allegations but seeking a divorce on other facts, and the petitioner does not dispute the cross-petition, the divorce is not treated as defended and the special procedure can be adopted.

applying for 'directions for trial'

The court sends a copy of the respondent's acknowledgment of service to the petitioner, who can then apply for 'directions for trial' – that is, make a written request that the case be heard.

The petitioner must complete and lodge with the court one copy of a form 'Request for directions for trial (special procedure)' and an affidavit in support, with the copy of the acknowledgment of service attached. The appropriate documents are normally sent to the petitioner by the court office when it has received the acknowledgment of service from the respondent. You should fill in only the top part of the request form: the name of the court, the number assigned to the petition, the names of the petitioner and respondent; then date and sign it. The rest of the form is completed by the registrar and court staff.

affidavits

The affidavit is a fairly straightforward document, mostly in the form of a questionnaire. The questions refer to the petition, asking for confirmation that its contents are true, and for any alterations or additions.

There is a different affidavit of evidence for each of the five facts on which a divorce can be based. If you want to rely on two facts – for example, unreasonable behaviour and adultery – two affidavits would have to be completed.

affidavit on adultery

You are asked to state the facts on which you base the allegation of adultery. If the co-respondent's name or identity is not known, this should be stated.

If the respondent has admitted the adultery on the acknowledgment of service or by making a written statement, you should identify the respondent's signature on the document, which should be sent with the affidavit; similarly, where the co-respondent has admitted the adultery.

You should give all the firsthand information available, such as the date of confession of adultery or details of circumstances that tend to show that the respondent has committed adultery. You may need to supply further affidavits by other people who can give corroborative information.

You also have to confirm that you find it intolerable to live with the respondent.

affidavit on unreasonable behaviour
Further evidence to substantiate any allegations made in the petition may have to be given. But there is no need for a blow-by-blow account of every incident provided the respondent's conduct has been adequately set out in the petition. If the registrar is not satisfied with the information, he will call for further evidence to be supplied, such as a medical report or a witness's affidavit.

affidavit on desertion
The date on which desertion began has to be given, and you must state that you did not agree to the separation and that he or she did not offer to return.

affidavit on separation
Where husband and wife have been living in separate households for the whole of the years apart, the relevant dates and separate addresses should be given, and when and why you decided that the marriage was at an end. Merely living apart is not necessarily sufficient; the separation starts from the time you considered the marriage had broken down.

Where husband and wife continued living in the same household because it was impossible or impracticable to live completely apart although the marriage was at an end, the court may nevertheless accept this as separation. But, in such a case, you must give the fullest possible information about the separateness of the households. (If the space provided in the standard affidavit form is inadequate, attach an extra sheet dealing with this point.) The less the contact has been between husband and wife, the more likely is the court to regard the couple as separated.

You should have had as little to do with each other as possible: eaten and slept separately, preferably each cooked your own meals, looked after your own clothes and accommodation. If the registrar is still in doubt about the circumstances, he may remove the case from the special procedure list, to be heard in open court, so that fuller evidence can be given. (If this happens, you may need to consult a solicitor; you can apply for legal aid if your financial position makes you eligible.)

In a divorce with consent, the petitioner must state in the affidavit that the signature on the acknowledgment of service form is that of the respondent. This signature proves the respondent's consent to the divorce. You must return with the affidavit the copy of the respondent's acknowledgment of service form sent by the court.

swearing the affidavit
An affidavit is sworn by taking it to a commissioner for oaths or a solicitor (but not the one acting for the person making the affidavit) or the court office. There is no fee for swearing an affidavit before a court official; a solicitor or commissioner for oaths makes a small charge (at present, £3 plus 75p per attachment, called an exhibit).

When the completed affidavit has been signed and sworn, it has to be sent or taken to the court with the application form requesting directions for trial.

registrar giving directions

When the registrar is satisfied that there is sufficient evidence to support the petition, he gives directions for the case to be dealt with under the special procedure and certifies that the petitioner is entitled to a decree nisi of divorce (or the decree of judicial separation).

However, if the registrar is not satisfied, he may invite the petitioner (or a witness) to file a further affidavit or to give additional information on the points the registrar is concerned about.

If the registrar still does not accept that there is sufficient evidence for a divorce, he may direct that the petition be removed from the special procedure list. A fresh application then has to be made for directions and for a date to be fixed for a hearing in open court before a judge.

getting back together
Some couples, once the divorce procedure is well under way, find that there is a chance of saving the marriage but feel they are bound to

continue with the court action to the end. This is not necessary. If you think at any stage that you and your husband/wife might like to give the marriage another try, say so to your solicitor or to the court. The proceedings can be adjourned or withdrawn.

You may want to consider whether some or all of the differences with your spouse can be resolved with outside, non-legal, help. A fresh viewpoint can often help. Such help can be obtained from a marriage guidance council or a conciliation service (your citizens advice bureau will know where such agencies are). The emphasis nowadays is on conciliation – trying to help the parties to resolve as many problems as possible by mutual agreement or mediation.

certificate of satisfaction about children

At the stage of giving directions for trial, if there is no dispute as to the arrangements for the children, the registrar fixes a date for the judge to decide whether the arrangements proposed are satisfactory. This is usually, but not necessarily, on the same day as the decree nisi is to be pronounced.

No final decree can be made where there are relevant children unless the judge has certified his satisfaction declaring

- that the arrangements that have been made for every relevant child are satisfactory or are the best that can be devised under the circumstances
  or
- that it is impracticable for the parents to make such arrangements (for instance, if the children are living abroad)
  or
- that there are circumstances making it desirable that the decree should be granted or made absolute without delay, even though the judge is unable to make the required declaration about the children. One parent (or both) must give the court a satisfactory undertaking to bring the question of the arrangements for the children before the court within a time specified by the judge.

In most cases where there are difficulties about the arrangements for the children, these must be sorted out before the decree nisi can be made absolute.

decree nisi and decree absolute

The decree nisi is a provisional decree and does not dissolve the marriage. It entitles the one who was the petitioner to apply to the court for the decree to be made absolute after six weeks have elapsed. Until this is done, you are still married.

The form of application for the decree nisi to be made absolute has to be obtained from the court office; it should be completed and returned to the court. There is no fee.

A decree can be made absolute earlier than the six weeks if the petitioner applies for this when the decree nisi is pronounced and attends to explain to the judge in person the reason for the application. The respondent must be given notice of this application by the petitioner. Such an application might be granted, for example, to enable one of the couple to marry again before a child is born.

If the petitioner does not apply for the decree nisi to be made absolute when the time comes, after a further three months have elapsed (that is, 19 weeks after the decree nisi), the one who was the respondent may apply to the registrar for the decree to be made absolute, with an affidavit setting out the reasons why he or she is applying.

The certificate making the decree absolute is sent by the court office to both parties. From the date on it, the marriage is at an end in law. Keep this certificate carefully; it will have to be produced if you want to marry again. Make a note of the name of the court, the reference number of the case and the date of the decree.

Some overseas countries do not like the relative informality of our decrees absolute, so if you are planning to live outside the UK, you may need a certified copy of the decree absolute, signed by the registrar and stamped by the court, which may be more easily accepted.

Getting an undefended divorce by special procedure

A table showing who acts at what stage and the documents involved is on pages 210 to 213 of this book.

Arrangements for the children

Where there are relevant children, the judge must have declared his satisfaction about the arrangements for them before a decree can be made absolute. Any decree made absolute without the judge's certifying his satisfaction about the arrangements for the children is void.

conciliation

Where you have difficulty in coming to an agreement about the children, it may help you to use a conciliation agency.

The service is there to help the two of you come to your own arrangements over the children. (Sometimes, if you get to court, the registrar or judge will encourage an attempt at conciliation to avoid a legal fight. A number of courts provide mediation facilities on the court premises.)

In an increasing number of areas, there is a family conciliation service for parents to help resolve disputes, whether or not they have started divorce proceedings. Many are affiliated to the National Family Conciliation Council (secretary at Llanberis, Brooklands Way, East Grinstead, West Sussex RH19 1DE). The local court or citizens advice bureau will be able to tell you if there is a conciliation service in your area, or you can write to the NFCC (enclose stamped addressed envelope for reply).

The function of the conciliator is to bring the parents together and assist them to work out a solution of their difficulties which will be mutually acceptable. In other words, the activity is one of mediation, with no pressure exercised and no solution imposed.

These services deal mainly with disputes over children but may also be able to achieve outline agreement in financial matters. Although financial or property matters are the province of the legal profession, in many cases involving children such matters are inextricably linked (for example, over the matrimonial home or payment of school fees), and where this is so, the parents and their solicitors, plus the conciliator, should work together.

custody, care and control

In the petition, the petitioner can request custody of any children of the family, and the respondent is asked in the acknowledgment of service whether he or she objects and wishes to make an application for custody on his or her own account.

Custody is a legal term indicating the right to make major, long-term, decisions for a child, mainly connected with education, medical care, moral and religious upbringing of the child, marriage. The parent having **care and control** is the one with whom a child lives, who has the right to make the practical everyday decisions about the child.

An order for joint custody may be suitable where the parents are able sensibly to discuss the upbringing of the child and are likely to remain able to do so.

Generally, the mother gets the care and control of young children. It tends to be assumed, particularly with very young children, that the mother can provide better for their emotional and physical needs and day-to-day care than the father, and that he should continue to be the breadwinner and pay for maintenance of the children.

It is open to the father to produce evidence to show that these factors do not apply so strongly in his particular case, or that there are other factors outweighing these – such as the mother's mental health or ability to care for the child. He may have to show that the mother is not a fit person to look after even her own child. Medical or social evidence may show that the child's need for the father is greater than his or her need for the mother, or that the father can fulfil the needs of the child better than the mother. The older the child, particularly if a boy, the less the mother's advantage. A father who wants to have care and control of his children usually has to prove that he has suitable accommodation for them and that he can make adequate arrangements for the children to be looked after if he is working (perhaps by his cohabitee or a paid housekeeper or a relative).

Courts tend to avoid splitting up the children and the length of time that a child has been with one or other parent is taken into account. In the absence of evidence that the child is being harmed in some way, courts generally do not want to interfere with arrangements that have worked well for some time, particularly if the change would mean a change in education.

Whatever form a custody order takes, should there be a dispute between the parents about the upbringing of the child, this can be brought to the court to be resolved.

access

The parent who does not have care and control of the child has the right to see the child – that is, for the child to have access to that parent – unless there are very strong reasons why it would be detrimental to the child.

It is normally assumed that access to the parent not having the care of the child is in the child's best interests, and very strong evidence (probably psychiatric) would be required to persuade a court not to order access.

An access order may provide for staying with the parent or just visiting, or a combination of both, as seems most appropriate in view of the distances involved, the relationships between the children and each parent, availability of accommodation, and any other relevant factors.

Courts usually make an order for 'reasonable access' and leave the parents to sort out the arrangements between them. Where the parents cannot sort out their own terms and there is a dispute, everything has to be worked out in detail and the court order can define when and where access should take place.

The order may be quite specific, dealing with precise days for access between specified times, laying down who shall call for and return the children, whether the visits shall be supervised, and sometimes dealing with payment of travelling expenses and also placing restrictions on the children being brought into contact with a cohabitee.

In the majority of cases, in practice, the parents ignore the order after a few months and make their own arrangements.

You and your (ex-)spouse will inevitably have to cope with changes in access for years to come. It is better to make these changes by agreement, rather than keep returning to court – and to get into the habit of reaching agreement as soon as possible.

appointment with judge

Both parents are notified by the court of the date when the judge will consider the arrangements proposed for the children. This is often on the same day as the decree nisi is to be pronounced. (When the petition is for judicial separation, the children's appointment must precede the pronouncement of the decree.)

The petitioner normally has to attend and the respondent must do so if the children will be living with him or her, or if there is an application for joint custody. Some courts require both parents to attend in any event to see if there are any problems that require sorting out.

Take to the appointment at the court a copy of the petition and of the statement of the proposed arrangements, and also any relevant documents, such as a copy of any previous court order for custody.

The hearing is in chambers – that is, in a court room in private – and is relatively informal, with the judge and clerk, the parents and their legal advisers (if any) and perhaps the court welfare officer present. The judge may ask questions about any points – for instance, he will want to know that there are proper arrangements for the children to see the other parent; that adequate financial provision is being made for the children; that the children get on reasonably well with any cohabitee of the parent with whom they will live.

If the judge is satisfied, he makes any necessary orders and records his satisfaction on the file before him and on the orders that go to the parents.

If the judge is not satisfied, he adjourns the hearing and may ask for further information or for a report from the court welfare officer.

Using a solicitor

'Do-it-yourself' divorce is relatively easy, but where the financial arrangements and division of property and assets are likely to pose problems, or where there is disagreement about custody or access for children, a solicitor's help will almost certainly be needed. Some advice on the financial aspects from a solicitor specialising in divorce problems is worthwhile, if only to avoid giving up rights in ignorance.

If you can sort out your financial affairs as equal partners, so much the better. However, one of you may be in a stronger financial position and have a stronger personality than the other. In such a case, it may not be possible for the two of you to achieve a fair agreement on your own. One or other of you may need to consult a solicitor to negotiate on your behalf.

But consulting a lawyer will involve you in expense, which may be out of proportion to anything gained. Win or lose, the higher the costs the less there is left for you, your spouse and children to share.

When faced with a breakdown of your marriage, you are likely to be at your most emotional and irrational, at the very time when you need to take hold of yourself and try to be dispassionate. You should ask yourself what you are fighting for and why, before you go to obtain legal advice. If you do not, the financial cost of divorce may be considerably increased by legal costs.

conciliation
Many parts of the country have set up what is called a 'conciliation service'. The aim of this is to settle differences in a reasonable and civilised way about such things as custody of children or access to them, living accommodation, money, ownership of goods. Use of such a service can help you avoid bitter arguments about these matters through lawyers or in the court itself. The people offering this service are specially trained in giving this kind of help, and are independent in the sense that they do not 'belong' to one side or the other nor do they 'act for' the court.

why are you going to a solicitor?

Most people are not quite sure what they want from a solicitor. On the one hand, they want a fair and detached legal adviser, and on the other hand they want a knight in shining armour, a champion to wage war against their husband or wife.

Before you go to a solicitor, ask youself 'what do I expect?'. Do not go for the following reasons:

★ not for emotional support

Solicitors are often used as a shoulder to cry on. The one-to-one relationship, and client confidentiality, make them uniquely available for unburdening the soul. Many solicitors are very understanding and can be of great help at this time. But beware of reaching the stage where your solicitor becomes an emotional prop and you are not really telephoning to discuss the case but for personal reassurance. Apart from any other dangers, solicitors' time costs money: their job is to deal primarily with the legal aspects of your case.

★ not in search of miracles

There is no such thing as a magic answer. In many cases, there is not much room to manoeuvre: it is usually just a question of trying to make the best of what money and property there is.

★ not for revenge

Are you really fighting for money and who is going to have the furniture? If you are just looking for another battle in your domestic war by which to hurt your spouse, you will probably end up more embittered and probably substantially out of pocket as well.

In some ways, having no idea what you want a solicitor for is as dangerous as going for revenge or for emotional support. It is often difficult for solicitors to know how to resolve a case if they have no idea of what the client's expectations are. The case may just drift on aimlessly, nobody really knowing what they are after, while costs are being run up.

what a solicitor can do for you

A solicitor should discuss your position dispassionately and advise you from the benefit of his experience what is likely to happen. Good advice early on may prevent matters becoming complicated or one party getting less than his or her entitlement, and can generally take the heat out of a situation.

● get you your divorce

Divorce by the special procedure is easy enough to do without a solicitor, but where the other spouse is wholly unreasonable or flatly refuses to co-operate in any way, a solicitor would be useful.

● help to get agreement about finances

There are cases where, whatever you do, you are faced with a long uphill battle to get financial information out of your husband or wife. However much you want to be reasonable over things, the other one may not wish to play ball, and may refuse to disclose assets.

Both of you will eventually have to swear affidavits of means and will get to know each other's financial position. So, withholding information at the early stages does nothing but run up costs and reduce the amount that there is to go round. If you go to see a solicitor over these problems, your spouse may then do so, too. Good solicitors will impress upon both of you the need to co-operate.

Your resources may leave very limited room for manoeuvre and therefore there may be little point in fighting it out in court. If money disputes cannot be settled and they run on for months or even years, the costs can run into thousands of pounds even where small amounts are in dispute. There is no point in getting your solicitor to try to push for more if the cost of getting it is going to be more than the amount you are asking for. The 'law of diminishing returns' applies: obtaining, or avoiding having to pay, the last £s of maintenance can become disproportionately expensive in terms of the extra legal costs incurred.

● sort out problems over children

Protracted litigation over the children is harmful to the children, harmful to you, and rarely produces a satisfactory result. Moreover, contested custody and access disputes can be extremely expensive. Avoid this wherever possible by asking your solicitor to refer your case to a conciliation service. This will give you and your partner the chance to reach an agreement over the future of the children before the case comes before the court.

● deal with requests for maintenance and division of property

The solicitor should know the appropriate court (magistrates' court, county court, divorce county court, High Court) for the particular order you require, and the procedure for applying.

Even in a simple case, an hour's legal advice may be worth its weight in gold. For example, although you may have reached broad agreement over how you are going to split your finances, a solicitor may be able to

★ put an agreement into wording that is clear and will be acceptable to the court

★ arrange maintenance and the division of property in an efficient way from a tax point of view

★ draw up a 'clean break' settlement, where appropriate, in such a way that it really cannot be reopened

★ point out things that you have not thought of: for example, that a wife may be losing substantial widow's pension rights under her husband's occupational pension scheme

★ take into account the effect of any proposed order on supplementary benefit entitlement.

A solicitor acts for one party only, and his professional duty is to act in that person's best long-term interest. Solicitors do not necessarily define 'best interest' as meaning 'most money'.

how to find a solicitor

Should you decide to consult a solicitor, choose one who is experienced in matrimonial work. This may rule out the solicitor whom you have previously dealt with, perhaps about buying the house or making your will. On the other hand, that solicitor may have a partner in the same firm who specialises in divorce matters, to whom you can be referred. But if the firm has acted for one or both of a couple in the past, there may be a policy of acting for neither in a matrimonial dispute.

Ask acquaintances who have been divorced whom they used. A recommendation can be a guide, but find out whether the friend who was so satisfied had the same kind of problems as you have.

The Law Society's regional directories of solicitors are available in citizens advice bureaux, public libraries and court offices throughout the country. Each directory lists solicitors practising in the area who have given information about their availability, whether they are willing to undertake legal aid cases and/or give fixed-fee interviews, and indicating the categories of work they have experience in (look for the category 'family').

fixed-fee interview
Under a scheme operated by the Law Society, solicitors are prepared to give a 'fixed-fee' interview: half-an-hour's legal advice for £5 (no extra for VAT). This is available to everyone, irrespective of financial means. Not all solicitors offer 'fixed-fee' interviews, so ask when making the appointment.

choosing the solicitor
When you telephone or write to a firm of solicitors asking for an appointment, say that you wish to be advised in connection with your matrimonial difficulties, and ask if they have a solicitor specialising in divorce and related financial matters, perhaps one who is a member of the Solicitors Family Law Association.

The Solicitors Family Law Association is an association of matrimonial lawyers who subscribe to a code of practice which is designed to encourage and assist parties to reconcile differences and wherever possible to avoid conflict. You can ask the secretary of the SFLA (154 Fleet Street, London EC4A 2HX) for a list of members in your region.

Extracts from the
Solicitors Family Law Association's
CODE OF PRACTICE

General

1.1. The solicitor should endeavour to advise, negotiate and conduct proceedings in a manner calculated to encourage and assist the parties to reconcile their differences and should inform the client of the approach he intends to adopt.

1.2. The solicitor should encourage the client to see the advantage to the family of a conciliatory rather than a litigious approach as a way of resolving the disputes. The solicitor should explain to the client that in nearly every case where there are children, the attitude of the client to the other party in any negotiations will affect the family as a whole and may affect the relationship of the children with the parents.

1.3. The solicitor should encourage the attitude that a family dispute is not a contest in which there is one winner and one loser, but rather a search for fair solutions. He should avoid using words or phrases that imply a dispute when no serious dispute necessarily exists, for example 'opponent', 'win', 'lose', or '*Smith v Smith*'. . . . .

1.6. The solicitor should aim to avoid or dispel suspicion or mistrust between parties, by encouraging at an early stage where possible, full frank and clear disclosure of information and openness in dealings.

1.7. The solicitor should aim to achieve settlement of differences as quickly as may be reasonable whilst recognising that the parties may need time to come to terms with their new situation.

Relationship with client

2.1. As a rule the solicitor should explain to the client at the outset the terms of his retainer and take care to ensure that the client is fully aware of the impact of costs on any chosen course of action. The solicitor should thereafter at all stages have regard to the cost of negotiations and proceedings. . . . .

2.3. The solicitor should create and maintain a relationship with his client of a kind which will preserve fully his independent judgement and avoid becoming so involved in the case that his own personal emotions may cloud his judgement.

2.4. Whilst recognising the need to advise firmly and guide the client the solicitor should ensure that where the decision is properly that of the client, it is taken by the client and that its consequences are fully understood, both as to its effect on any children involved and financially. . . . .

5.3. Where the purpose of taking a particular step in proceedings may be misunderstood the solicitor should consider explaining it in advance to the other party or his solicitors. . . . .

Children

6.2. The solicitor should, in advising, negotiating and conducting proceedings, assist both his client and the other parent to regard the welfare of the child as the first and paramount consideration.

6.3. The solicitor should aim to promote cooperation between parents in decisions concerning the child, both by formal arrangements (such as orders for joint custody); by practical arrangements (such as shared involvement in school events) and by consultation on important questions.

The guidelines set out in this Code cannot be absolute rules in as much as the solicitor may have to depart from them if the law or his professional obligations so require. They are a restatement of principles, objectives and recommendations which many solicitors practising family law already seek to follow and to which they seek to aspire in serving their clients.

October 1983

how solicitors charge

Solicitors basically charge by the hour, so that every interview, every telephone call, every letter and indeed every time the solicitor opens your file, means additional expense to you, the client. Inevitably, the longer the case goes on for, the greater will be the expense.

There is no reason why you should not ask what the solicitor's hourly rates or 'charge-out' rates are at the first interview.

Value added tax is payable on solicitors' fees and there will be additional costs such as court fees, fees of any barristers engaged and, if there are major areas of dispute over the value of items of property, valuer's fees as well.

A solicitor's hourly charge may be anything from £30 plus VAT in a provincial firm, whereas in London it may be from £50 per hour plus VAT, and in really upmarket firms, charge-out rates of £100 an hour plus VAT are not uncommon. So, using your solicitor as an emotional prop rather than as a legal adviser can turn out to be an extremely expensive luxury.

Where there is dispute over custody, or maintenance and property, it is likely that both parties will have a solicitor (and perhaps barristers). There will therefore be two bills to pay at the end of the case.

It matters not who 'wins' or 'loses' and who gets an order for costs against whom: the two sets of legal fees will have to be paid out of the same source – the parties' joint assets.

In many cases, solicitors deliver interim bills 'on account' at various stages. This helps the client to know where he stands, and paying as the case proceeds may avoid having to find a large amount at the end.

costs
You can ask, in the petition, that costs be paid by the other party. If the registrar makes an order for costs, your ex-spouse will be required to pay your costs, but only such as are 'necessary or proper for the attainment of justice' – known as party-and-party costs – usually about 75% to 80% of your solicitor's total bill. Even if there is an order for costs, therefore, there will still be a balance for you to pay.

Party-and-party costs (the costs recoverable from the other party if the court so orders) consist of the solicitor's fee for his professional services (known as 'profit costs'): in effect, payment for time involved in dealing with the case, plus VAT. Also included are the reasonable out-of-pocket expenses (normally called 'disbursements') which your solicitor has had to pay on your behalf: principally, court fees, the fee for a copy marriage certificate, travelling expenses and possibly barrister's fee.

When seeking advice from solicitors

- Do not hesitate to ask the solicitor to explain and discuss any points about which you are not clear.
- Be prepared to listen to your solicitor and do not assume that cautious advice is necessarily lack of enthusiasm.
- Remember that you can accept or reject advice as you wish. But before you reject advice, make sure that you understand the point.
- Do not leave it to your solicitor to do everything: the more time he or she spends on the case, because of the time basis of costing, the higher the bill is going to be. There is much work that can be done by you yourself that will save solicitors' costs—but tell your solicitor what you are doing.
- You are entitled to be told how the litigation is progressing and, in particular, how much it is costing at any stage.
- Ask if you qualify for legal advice and assistance under the green form scheme, and/or for legal aid. This will depend on your financial circumstances.

The limits for financial eligibility for legal advice and legal aid are reviewed by the government each year, and changes come into effect in November.

The green form scheme

The basic idea behind the legal advice and assistance scheme (referred to generally as the 'green form scheme' because of the colour of the application form) is to allow people who would not otherwise be able to afford it to get some legal advice. You may be required to pay a contribution, depending on your income and capital.

The scheme entitles you to up to £50-worth of legal advice in the first instance (£75 if the solicitor helps to draft the divorce petition). The solicitor's hourly rate for 'green form' work is £25, so you can get two or three hours' worth.

Work the solicitor may do under the green form advice and assistance scheme relevant to money and divorce includes

★ general advice on whether there are grounds for divorce or judicial separation
★ advice on questions of domicile
★ proving the validity of a foreign marriage
★ advice on the procedure of getting a divorce
★ drafting the petition and the documents to accompany the petition
★ advising a respondent on defending the divorce and the implications of doing so
★ help with an application for legal aid
★ advice on obtaining an injunction
★ registration of a land charge on the matrimonial home
★ advice about custody, care and control of and access for children
★ advice about maintenance, and arrangements concerning the matrimonial home
★ correspondence or discussions with solicitors acting for the other party to try to negotiate a settlement.

A separate green form could cover

★ correspondence with building societies, hire purchase and finance companies and public utilities with regard to problems about payment of bills, instalments or other debts following the breakdown of a marriage
★ advice on supplementary benefit entitlement and other welfare rights.

The one thing a solicitor cannot do under the green form scheme is actually to conduct the case on your behalf, or to appear for you in the divorce court. However, for a hearing in the magistrates' court (in connection with maintenance or an injunction perhaps), the solicitor can apply to the legal aid area office for approval to represent his client in that court.

The green form scheme is appropriate for simple undefended divorces or for negotiating straightforward settlements. When the initial limit of £50 or £75 is used up, the solicitor can apply to the Law Society's legal aid area office to extend the limit. One request for an extension is usually granted.

The solicitor carries out the assessment there and then, and can tell you straightaway whether you are eligible for the green form scheme.

On a green form application, all that happens is that when you go to the solicitor's office, he or she ascertains your financial eligibility on the figures provided by you. The solicitor will then fill in and ask you to sign the appropriate form.

Only one green form can be completed covering all matters 'arising from proceedings for divorce or judicial separation'. This means that the applicant is not entitled to £50-worth (or £75-worth, as the case may be) of green form assistance for each matter connected with the divorce – the divorce itself, maintenance, custody and injunctions. There is only one green form for all that (an application can be made for an extension of the cost limit). If, however, there are other matters, such as housing or supplementary benefit, hire purchase debts, or whatever, each of those can form the subject of a separate green form application and entitle the person to, in the first instance, £50-worth of advice.

eligibility for the green form scheme

Eligibility for the green form scheme is based on financial limits. The solicitor will have to ask about savings and other capital and about your gross weekly income, your outgoings and any dependants. He enters these details on the green form.

capital

Your disposable capital must not exceed £730, or £930 if you have one dependant, £1,050 if two dependants, increasing by £60 for each additional dependant. The value of your home and its contents, personal clothing and tools of trade are not counted as part of disposable capital.

Anyone receiving supplementary benefit or family income supplement is automatically eligible for the green form scheme, subject to the disposable capital threshold. So, someone getting supplementary benefit but who has savings of, say, £2,000 would be ineligible for the green form scheme.

income

Disposable income is the income after deduction of tax and national insurance contributions and minus £30.68 for a dependent spouse and minus an allowance for dependent children of £13.73 (under age 11) or £20.55 (age 11 to 15) or £24.75 (age 16 and 17), and minus £32.17 for an adult dependant. The income of the spouse is not included where husband and wife have a contrary interest in the case at issue. This means that often the non-working wife of even a very wealthy man is eligible for the green form scheme.

The disposable income limit is £103 in the last seven days (plus the allowance for dependants).

contribution

If your disposable income is £49 or less per week, you will not be required to pay any contribution but if it is between £49 and £103, a contribution will be required from you. This is a single payment, on a scale from £5 up to £57.

It is probably worthwhile to get advice under the green form scheme even if you have to pay a high contribution because the cost of legal advice will undoubtedly be more if you pay privately, and under the green form scheme you will be exempt from court fees.

If you are eligible, you will have to sign the green form, confirming that the information given is correct and that you accept the terms of the scheme. If your disposable income is high enough for you to have to pay a contribution, you will be asked to pay the appropriate amount to the solicitor straightaway (but you may be allowed to pay in instalments).

The legal aid scheme

Where there is likely to be any contest, or a hearing in court, the green form scheme would not be adequate but you can apply for a legal aid certificate.

Under the legal aid scheme, which is funded by the state and administered by the Law Society, an eligible applicant gets the services of a solicitor (and barrister, where appropriate) free, or on payment of an assessed contribution towards the cost.

Legal aid is available for applications in a divorce court relating to any maintenance orders, property orders, lump sum orders and contested arrangements for children. Legal aid is not normally available for an undefended divorce by the special procedure.

The solicitor can supply the application form for legal aid. The form requires details of the applicant, his wife or her husband and children, and a summary of the applicant's case. It is not all that straightforward to complete; the solicitor will help you with the form, but he can charge you for this (unless you are eligible for advice under the green form scheme).

The application is sent to the secretary of the legal aid area office for consideration of the legal merits of your case and to the legal aid assessment officer of the Department of Health and Social Security to assess what contribution is required. You will be sent a 12-page financial statement form to complete. On this you will have to give full details of yourself, your home; your regular income from investments and work; your valuables and savings. There is also a form for your employer to complete.

financial eligibility for legal aid

As with the green form scheme, the criteria are the amount of disposable income and of disposable capital. If either is above the limit, you are ineligible for legal aid.

In a matrimonial dispute, the spouse's income or capital can be ignored for all calculations of disposable income and disposable capital.

income

Disposable income is net of tax and national insurance contributions, but including child benefit and any maintenance (net of tax) received under a court order or agreement from your spouse.

From this will be deducted
★ expenses incurred in connection with employment (such as fares to work, trade union membership dues) and child-minding costs
★ rent, or mortgage repayments
★ rates
★ HP commitments
★ insurance commitments
★ maintenance paid to spouse from whom you are living apart
★ allowance for dependants: if you and your spouse are living together, £1,595 is deducted from annual income for wife, and for each dependent child £714 to £1,673, depending on ages.

A contribution towards your costs will be required unless your disposable income is less than £2,050. The most you can be asked to pay by way of contribution is one-quarter of the amount (25p for every £) by which your disposable income is above £2,050 and under £4,925, up to a maximum of £718.75.

disposable income

if under £2,050 a year	'free' legal aid i.e. no contribution (provided capital also within 'free' limit)
if between £2,050 and £4,925	contribution required (25% of excess over £2,050)
£4,925	upper limit for legal aid

capital

For disposable capital, ignored are
★ value of the house you live in
★ value of any other property or money that is in dispute between you and your spouse
★ furniture, personal clothing, tools of trade, car.

Apart from this, virtually everything that is capable of being valued in money terms will count as disposable capital: not merely cash or deposits or shares but sums that could be borrowed on the security of insurance policies. Also counted in are furs and jewellery (other than engagement or wedding ring), antiques and other valuables.

Where the capital assets come to between £3,000 and £4,500, you will have to contribute a lump sum equal to the capital above £3,000 (this means a maximum of £1,500). This payment is additional to any contribution that has to be made because of your income. If the contribution you are asked to make seems to be unreasonably high in relation to the likely cost of your case, you can ask for a reassessment.

disposable capital

if under £3,000	'free' legal aid i.e. no contribution (provided income also within 'free' limit)
if between £3,000 and £4,500	contribution required (on excess over £3,000)
£4,500	upper limit for legal aid

(The figures given here came into effect in November 1983.)

waiting for the decision

The average wait before knowing whether a legal aid certificate will be issued is seven weeks, but the waiting time may run into several months.

A legal aid certificate cannot cover work done before the date the certificate is issued. Effectively this means that your case will come to a halt once an application for legal aid has been made, because the Law Society is unlikely to allow any further extensions on a green form and, by now, the costs limit of the green form scheme is likely to have been reached.

emergency legal aid

In cases of real emergency (for example, an application for an injunction), a legal aid certificate can be granted almost immediately. You have to fill in a special pink form (which the solicitor will provide) explaining why the application is urgent.

If it is granted, you must thereafter apply for and provide all the details for getting a full legal aid certificate (even if you do not want to take the case any further). If you do not, you will yourself have to meet the costs incurred under the emergency certificate.

the offer and contributions

If the decision is that you are eligible and no contribution is required, a legal aid certificate is sent to you and to your solicitor.

If a contribution is required, you are sent an offer setting out details of the amount required and how you will be expected to pay it. Contributions based on income normally have to be paid by 12 monthly instalments; the capital sum there and then.

The legal aid certificate will not be issued until after you have accepted the offer and made the first of the monthly contributions and any lump sum payment. It is important to keep up monthly payments and to carry out the conditions of the legal aid certificate (such as informing the legal aid office of any changes in your financial situation, perhaps because of maintenance payments). If you do not, you run the risk of your certificate being withdrawn and finding yourself liable for your legal costs.

No work done by the solicitor before the legal aid certificate was issued is covered. The solicitor is entitled to charge you for any pre-certificate work and you will have to pay (unless the work was carried out under the green form scheme). Once a legal aid certificate is granted, the solicitor must act in every way as for a fee-paying client.

if your income or capital changes

If your disposable income increases by more than £500 per annum, or decreases by more than £250 per annum in the twelve months following the assessment, you must inform the Law Society via your solicitor (for example, if a maintenance order is made while property and custody matters are still being contested).

You will be reassessed and your contribution may be adjusted or the certificate 'discharged' (that is, ended).

If there is an increase in income later than twelve months after the first assessment, the Law Society can order a reassessment only with a view to discharging a certificate, not to change the contribution required.

As far as disposable capital is concerned, you are supposed to report increases of £120 or more. You may be called upon to pay another lump sum contribution or the certificate may be taken away if you are now over the capital limit.

If you acquire property or money as a result of the proceedings, this is unlikely to result in a reassessment because the money or property will probably have been part of the subject matter of the dispute.

legal fees when on legal aid

When a person is granted legal aid, he or she ceases to become personally responsible for his or her own legal fees. The solicitor should not bill them direct from then on for work within the limits of the legal aid certificate. Fees of solicitors and barristers and any other disbursements during the existence of the certificate, will be paid by the Law Society.

Many people think that because they are legally aided, they are not going to pay anything. But they may be required to contribute to the cost of those fees, not only by paying a contribution as a condition of receiving legal aid but by being required to make good any shortfall on the legal aid fund out of any property recovered or preserved in the proceedings. This is the statutory legal aid charge or 'first charge'.

the statutory charge

The statutory charge is intended to recoup some of the taxpayer's money which finances the legal aid fund.

When the legal aid fund has to pay out more than it collects by way of contribution from the 'assisted' (that is, the legally-aided) person and from any costs the other side is ordered to pay, it then has a first charge on any property recovered or preserved. That means any property which has been in issue in the proceedings or which has been recovered

or preserved under the terms of a compromise to avoid or bring an end
to proceedings.

'In the proceedings' means all proceedings in the same suit or action
for which legal aid was granted, not just those relating to the property
recovered or preserved. For example, if the legal aid certificate covered
the divorce, a custody application, an injunction and a transfer of
property order application, the cost of all those proceedings would be
part of the charge on the property transferred.

on property

Property could be a lump sum payment, the value of the house (or a
share of it) and any other asset that was transferred or handed over or
has been kept.

Property is held to have been recovered or preserved if it has been in
issue in the proceedings – that is, it has been the subject of a claim –
even if the case is settled halfway through without an order having been
made or an order is made based on agreement.

The only time when you can be certain that property would not be
regarded as 'in issue' would be where the matrimonial home was in
joint names, there was no dispute as to who should continue to occupy
it, there is no dispute as to the shares in which it will be distributed,
and no application has been made by either party (even in the prayer
to the petition) for a transfer of property order regarding the former
matrimonial home. What it effectively means, therefore, is that the only
way to be certain to avoid the former home being the subject of the
statutory charge is to agree at a very early stage, before proceedings
are commenced, as to what is to be done with the home.

Only if the property was genuinely never in dispute would there be no
risk of the statutory charge applying in the end. For example, if you
came to a final agreement before the application or if in correspondence
it had been conceded that the other party always had the property
rather than that it was now being transferred, this would be evidence
that there was no element of dispute. Ideally, if it could be achieved in
time, send an agreed statement with the application for legal aid, so
that the Law Society would know from the start there there was nothing
that would be gained or preserved through the proceedings.

exemption

In matrimonial proceedings, the first £2,500 of any property gained or preserved is exempt from the statutory charge, and the charge does not apply to any maintenance payments.

postponement and substitution

Where the property is a house and is being transferred rather than sold, the legally aided person to whom it has been transferred does not have to pay the statutory charge there and then. Instead, the charge is put on the house and is not enforced until the house is sold. No interest is payable.

The legal aid fund's postponement of enforcing the charge is relevant also when property has been preserved. For example, if the house belongs to the wife and the husband's application for a share in it does not succeed, the wife has preserved her ownership of the house and the statutory charge will be enforced, but only when she comes to sell the house.

When the house is being sold so that another one can be bought with the proceeds of sale, the legal aid fund may agree to put the charge on the substitute dwelling house, provided that

★ the net value of the new home covers the amount of the charge
  and
★ it is to be the sole residence of the assisted person and at least one unmarried child under 18 or in full-time education at the date of purchase of the substitute home, or it is necessary for the assisted person or his or her dependants to move for reasons of health, disability or employment
  and
★ the substitution is just and reasonable and a refusal would cause hardship to the assisted person.

Only in exceptional cases will substitution be allowed more than once.

The charge on property other than the home – for instance, a lump sum – can never be postponed. This would include a lump sum that arises out of the sale of a house.

examples of legal aid and the statutory charge

The legal aid charge 'bites' in sometimes unexpected circumstances, as the following fictitious and real-life examples show.

example 1

Husband and wife live in a council house. They have two children aged 5 and 7. H walks out on W and pays her no maintenance. W, who does not work, claims supplementary benefit and gets housing benefit. H contacts her, admits adultery, and asks for a divorce.

The wife goes to a solicitor for advice under the green form scheme (no contribution is required from her because she is on supplementary benefit) for help with her divorce petition and also advice on transferring the tenancy wholly to her. H does not agree to the transfer of the tenancy.

He becomes violent towards W and the children, and she has to apply for an injunction. H claims custody and causes difficulty over agreeing about access.

For all of these matters, the wife requires legal aid, which is granted with no contribution required. However many hundreds, or even thousands, of pounds are run up in legal fees on her behalf, she will never have to pay a penny to the legal aid fund, because no property on which any value can be placed has been 'recovered or preserved'. (The local authority tenancy has no value in this context.)

The husband applies for legal aid to defend the transfer of property application and the injunction and to apply for custody. He gets a legal aid certificate subject to a contribution. Win or lose, however, he will not be required to pay anything more towards his own costs.

The net result is that the legal aid fund ends up paying virtually the whole of both parties' costs.

example 2

The wife is legally aided with nil contribution. The couple's marriage has lasted over ten years and there are two children. They live in their own house which, after deducting the outstanding mortgage debt, is now worth £20,000.

The house was bought in the husband's name. The wife has worked throughout the marriage and has helped with the mortgage payments, so that it can be argued that she has a right to a share in the value of the house. She applies for a transfer of the whole house to herself; he applies for a transfer of her share to him. On the basis that she is prepared to forgo maintenance, the court orders that he should transfer the whole house to her.

The result of this is that the whole of the property has been in issue; she has 'recovered' her husband's share and 'preserved' whatever undefined share she had. Therefore, the statutory charge can be up to the full net value of the house (£20,000), minus the £2,500 which is exempt.

Unless she gets an order for costs against H, she will be liable to repay the legal aid fund for her full legal costs: not just the costs of the property transfer application but also those of any other proceedings which may have been taken under the certificate – such as a custody application – irrespective of the fact that she has not received any money out of which to meet the charge. However, the legal aid fund will not require payment until the house is sold.

example 3

The house was bought in joint names and, on divorce, the wife applies for a transfer to her of the husband's half share. She also applies for periodical payments, the amount of which the husband contests.

At the end of the hearing, the court makes an order for periodical payments as sought by her, and orders the husband to transfer his half share in the house to her. The result is that only the value of his interest in the house (say, £10,000) has been in issue and has been gained by the wife and therefore £7,500 is potentially chargeable (£10,000 less the exempt £2,500). Although the periodical payments do not count as a gain, the cost incurred in contesting them form part of the charge.

example 4

The house is in joint names, and there is no dispute between husband and wife as to the shares in which they are entitled to the proceeds of sale. The only dispute is that the husband wants the house sold immediately and the wife says that this will give her insufficient money to rehouse herself and the children. She applies for an order that the house should not be sold until the youngest child completes education. After a contested hearing, the court orders this.

In this situation, the charge will not apply to the proceeds of selling the matrimonial home when it is sold because nothing has been 'recovered' by the wife (she gets nothing in excess of her agreed half share) and nothing has been preserved because her share has never been under attack. The only thing that she has 'preserved' is her right to continue to occupy the matrimonial home, which is personal to her and has no inherent monetary value.

example 5

(based on the case of Hanlon v The Law Society)

The wife was granted a legal aid certificate. The former matrimonial home was in the husband's sole name but she probably had a right to a share by virtue of having contributed to the mortgage payments. She applied for and got an order that the home be transferred to her outright. He had initially defended the divorce, and applied for an order that such interest as she might have in the house should be transferred to him. Therefore, the whole of the matrimonial home was 'in issue'.

During the course of the protracted proceedings, her costs ran up to over £8,000, made up as follows:

divorce and injunction applications	£925
custody proceedings	£1,150
applications for maintenance and property adjustment orders	£5,950
	£8,025

The legal aid fund had a charge on all of the £8,025. The net value of the matrimonial home was at that time only £10,000, so all that the wife would get if the house were sold would be £2,500 (the exemption), the other £7,500 going towards the £8,025 charge. The husband was legally aided throughout but, because he neither preserved nor gained anything, the legal aid fund paid all his legal costs (except for the amount of the contribution he was required to make).

The real problem did not arise until the wife wanted to sell the house because it was proving too expensive to run. The legal aid fund did not (and still does not) enforce the charge on a matrimonial home when it is recovered by the legally-aided party until the property comes to be sold. The House of Lords held that she could sell the house, not pay the charge but use the money for buying a new house, and that the legal aid fund could take a substitute charge on the new property she bought.

example 6

(based on the case of Simmons v Simmons)

The wife, who was legally aided, was still living in the matrimonial home, the net value of which was £38,500. After protracted proceedings, having run up £8,000 of legal costs, an order was made for the house to be sold and out of the proceeds the wife to receive a lump sum of £26,750. It was a sum carefully arrived at to enable the wife to buy another home for herself and the children, with the aid of a further sum she could raise on mortgage. Apparently it did not occur to anybody at first that she would not get £26,750 at all, but only £18,750, because the legal aid charge would 'bite' as soon as the matrimonial home was sold and she got the lump sum. (The legal aid fund has no discretion to postpone the enforcement of a charge against cash.)

A practice direction has since been issued by the Divorce Registry requiring solicitors of legally aided clients to provide an estimate of their costs at the hearing so that the court can take account of the effect of the statutory charge.

Legal advice and/or legal aid

	'green form' scheme (legal advice and assistance)	legal aid scheme
who is eligible?	anyone with income not more than £103 p.w.† and with capital not more than £730‡	anyone with income not more than £4925 p.a.† and with capital not more than £4500‡
what does it cover?	advice, and help with documents up to £50-worth (@ hourly rate of £25) or £75-worth if solicitor drafts divorce petition	all legal work required including representation in court by solicitor and, if necessary, barrister
how long does it go on for?	until cost/time limit reached (but can apply for extension for further work)	until case concluded
how does one apply?	by giving information to solicitor about income and savings; he completes 'green form' if eligible	by giving information to solicitor to complete application form to pass on to area legal aid office, with details of grounds for case, and to DHSS assessment office with details of income, expenses and capital (unless receiving supplementary benefit)

how long does decision take?	solicitor decides there and then	weeks or months while assessment being made; solicitor will not start legal aid work until certificate issued (emergency certificate may be granted in urgent case)
what does it cost me?	if income between £49 and £103 p.w., contribution (from £5 to £57) payable there and then; can be paid in instalments where lump sum over £2500 gained, solicitor's charge taken from it	if income between £2050 and £4925 p.a., contribution payable by monthly instalments and if capital between £3000 and £4500, contribution payable when offer of legal aid is accepted on gain or preservation of property over £2500 where statutory charge arises, remaining legal costs of case taken from property recovered or preserved
	† contribution required if more than £49 p.w. ‡ higher if dependants	† contribution required if more than £2050 p.a. ‡ contribution required if more than £3000

legal aid costs

High legal costs can be run up over what may in essence be quite trivial disputes. Solicitors' duty to the legal aid fund requires them to report to the Law Society if they consider that the client is asking for litigation unreasonably – for example, by refusing to accept an offer of settlement.

Even though you are on legal aid, it is important to ask your solicitor to keep you posted on the costs of the case, particularly where the house or a lump sum is being negotiated for, and to explain to you what the statutory charge may entail in your case.

paying the charge

In legally aided cases, any money ordered by the court has to be paid to the solicitor because only he can give a receipt for it. He should pay it all into the legal aid fund, but if he undertakes that the cost of the case will not be more than £xxx, he can pay just that amount into the fund and the rest direct to the recipient. Otherwise, the recipient has to wait until the legal aid fund has settled up the costs before being paid the balance.

---

when going to a solicitor

Do ask yourself what you want from a lawyer
    take all relevant documents with you
    ask the solicitor what his/her hourly charging rate is
    give accurate information

Don't waste the solicitor's time by
    not having information ready
    not listening
    raising irrelevant or non-legal points
    raise objections just to get at your ex-partner
    think it's all free when you're getting legal aid
    expect miracles

Don't forget to find out whether you are eligible for the green form scheme and/or legal aid (have details of income and capital ready)

Remember to ask the solicitor for interim statements of how costs are building up.

Getting money before the divorce

If you are not at the stage of petitioning for divorce or judicial separation, you can apply to the local magistrates' court or the county court for an order for financial provision from your spouse.

through the county court

An application can be made to any county court for maintenance or a lump sum payment, even when no divorce is required or possible. The applicant has to satisfy the court that the other party has failed to provide reasonable maintenance for the applicant or for any child of the family.

An affidavit in support has to be submitted with details of the applicant's financial resources and needs. The respondent is required to file an affidavit in answer within 14 days of the service of the application upon him or her by the court. The county court registrar normally hears the application in chambers in the same way as an application for maintenance in divorce proceedings.

It is unlikely that you will be able to get a legal aid certificate for an application to the county court; the Law Society's *Notes for guidance* in the 1984 *Legal Aid handbook* say that 'Where the magistrates' court is able to provide the relief the client is seeking ... legal advisers will normally be expected to commence proceedings in the magistrates' court.'

through the magistrates' court

The magistrates' court can make orders for periodical payments for any amount and for lump sums of up to £500 each for the applicant and any children. The lump sum can be, for example, to repay the applicant for expenses reasonably incurred in maintaining herself or himself and the children during the period before the order was made.

You have to be able to prove that your spouse
* has deserted you, or
* has behaved in such a way that you cannot reasonably be expected to live with him or her, or
* has failed to provide reasonable maintenance for you or the children.

If you and your spouse have agreed about maintenance, you can go to the magistrates' court and ask for an agreed order to be made along those lines (provided the court thinks this reasonable) without the need for any grounds to be proved.

Being able to get an order in the magistrates' court is particularly useful where you do not propose to divorce in the immediate future but want a court order for maintenance for tax reasons.

The procedure for applying for a maintenance order in a magistrates' court is simple and costs relatively little; no affidavits are required. The application can be made to any magistrates' court in the area where either husband or wife lives, or where they last lived together. Legal aid (or approval for 'assistance by way of representation' under the green form scheme) can be applied for to make or defend such an application.

Both the applicant and the respondent will be asked to provide evidence about their income and expenditure and assets. Before making any order, the magistrates' court takes into account such factors as income and earning capacity, obligations and responsibilities, age, any physical disabilities, duration of the marriage, previous standard of living, the contribution each has made to the family.

The interval between applying to the magistrates' court and the hearing varies from court to court; it is likely to be between one and two months. In a case of urgent need, a court can be asked for an expedited hearing, or an interim order to tide the applicant over until such time as the case can be heard fully. An interim maintenance order lasts for a maximum of 3 months and may be extended for three months more.

If subsequently there is a petition for divorce, details of any magistrates' court order for maintenance have to be given on it, where information is asked about 'other proceedings in any court'.

through the divorce court

Once the petition has been lodged at the divorce county court, an application for an order for financial provision can be made there. If you have obtained an order for maintenance at the magistrates' court or county court, this remains in force until there is an order in the divorce county court.

maintenance pending suit

None of the long-term orders for maintenance can be made until the decree nisi and do not take effect until the decree has been made absolute. However, the court has power to order temporary maintenance payments for a spouse until the decree absolute. This is known as maintenance pending suit. The main point of the m.p.s. order is to keep the wife and children going until an order can be made after fuller examination of the overall financial position.

An application for maintenance pending suit can be made as soon as the petition is filed. It may take 3 to 6 weeks for the application to be heard. You will have to give the fullest possible information as to your needs and provide an affidavit of means, as should the respondent. If the respondent fails to file an affidavit of means, the registrar may make quite a high order: this may bring the respondent's financial affairs into the open more quickly if he wants to prove that the order is too high for him to manage.

Maintenance pending suit is in the nature of an interim order until the court has had an opportunity to consider fully the claim for financial provision. It comes into effect straightaway and lasts at most until the decree absolute.

from the state

When the marriage breaks up and you have separated, you may find that you need – and now qualify for – financial help from the state.

Most generally applicable is supplementary benefit for someone not in full-time work (which is defined as 30 hours a week or more) and family income supplement for someone who is at work and has at least one child.

Both supplementary benefit (SB) and family income supplement (FIS) are a 'passport' to various other benefits, such as free dental treatment, no prescription charges, free milk and vitamins for a child under 5, school meals without charge, and legal advice and assistance under the green form scheme and exemption from some court fees.

For either supplementary benefit or FIS, you have to apply to the DHSS (Department of Health and Social Security) on the appropriate forms, available from post offices, social security offices and citizens advice bureaux. The DHSS leaflet FB3, *Help for one-parent families,* summarises the cash and other benefits available.

supplementary benefit

You are not eligible for supplementary benefit if your capital or savings are more than £3,000 (but certain types of capital may be fully or partially ignored). For income, there is not one single threshold figure: it is based on the scale rate applying to the category of your personal status – married couples, single people, children according to age. The scale rate is meant to meet normal day-to-day living expenses (except housing costs); any additional requirements are taken into account for individual cases. The scale rate figures are revised by the government each year.

The DHSS calculate supplementary benefit by making a list of all the requirements a household has, and taking away the resources coming in. If your resources fall short of the scale rate requirements, supplementary benefit is payable to bring you up to your appropriate scale rate. After 52 weeks of receiving supplementary benefit without being required to be available for work, the 'long-term' rate comes into effect, which is considerably higher.

A lone parent with a child under 16 living with him or her can claim supplementary benefit without registering for work.

For an owner-occupier, the supplementary benefit will cover the interest element (not capital) of mortgage repayments, provided the DHSS do not think the house is too large; there is an allowance towards repairs and insurance.

Your 'resources' are all the money you have coming in, such as child benefit and earnings. Earnings are net, and allowance is made for such expenses as fares for getting to work and cost of child-minding. The first £4 a week of net earnings are disregarded and for lone parents there is an additional disregard of half of any net earnings between £4 and £20. So, a single parent whose net weekly earnings are £20 or more has a maximum disregard of £12 (net) per week.

Single payments for exceptional needs can also be requested by someone receiving supplementary benefit, but if you have capital over £500, you would be expected to use the excess before such a payment could be made. There are other fairly stringent provisions. But if the appropriate criteria are met, single payments can be received for various items such as essential furniture and household equipment, clothing, household repairs, maternity needs, expenses connected with looking for work. A citizens advice bureau can be asked for advice on this.

A claim form for supplementary benefit is in the DHSS leaflet SB1. The *Supplementary Benefits Handbook* is an annual guide to claimants' rights, published by HMSO (£2.50). The Child Poverty Action Group's *National Welfare Benefits Handbook* gives detailed information and advice (price £3). The DHSS leaflet FB2 *Which benefit?* tells you how to work out your entitlement to supplementary benefit and family income supplement.

supplementary benefit and court orders

Sometimes a court order is made for maintenance which just takes the wife out of her existing supplementary benefit entitlement. This means that she would lose her right to free school meals for the children, free prescriptions, and so on, and she would also lose the right to any special needs payments. Also, an order just taking the wife off supplementary benefit while she is still on the lower rate will do her out of the higher long-term rate possibly in a few weeks' time. This can be a real hardship to the wife – and often to the husband who may have been ordered to pay a bit more to his wife whereas, in fact, she receives less.

If a lump sum is ordered by the court, the amount may bring her above the capital limit, and supplementary benefit would cease, or the income which is assumed by the DHSS to derive from the lump sum may make her no longer eligible.

If a woman had to claim supplementary benefit because the husband is not paying the maintenance he was ordered to pay and the man eventually pays off the arrears, she will be asked to repay any supplementary benefit payments she had been receiving in the meantime.

After divorce, a man remains legally responsible for maintaining his children. If he does not do so and the mother has to claim supplementary benefit for them, the DHSS will try to get the man (if he can be located) to pay the amount they are giving out to the mother by way of benefit for the children. If he refuses, they can take him to court. (Although the man may be able to afford to pay more, he cannot be forced to do so by the DHSS. Moreover, every £1 he pays above the supplementary benefit figures for the children is deducted, £ for £, from the ex-wife's supplementary benefit payment.)

housing benefit

Any householder or joint householder receiving supplementary benefit qualifies for housing benefit. The DHSS notifies the local authority when someone comes on to supplementary benefit, and then the council

• **for an owner-occupier** credits the person's rates account with the amount of rates payable (i.e. the rates are 'paid' by a paper transaction)

• **for a council tenant** credits the person's rent and rates account with the amount due (another paper transaction). The tenant may still have to pay something – for example, if a charge for heating is payable with the rent, he may have to pay that out of his weekly supplementary benefit payment

• **for a private tenant** the council credits the rates account, and sends the tenant a girocheque for the amount of his rent (in certain circumstances, it can be paid directly to the landlord).

Someone just above supplementary benefit eligibility may qualify for a housing benefit supplement to help towards housing costs.

SHAC (189a Old Brompton Road, London SW5 0AR) publishes three guides to housing benefit: one for council tenants, one for home owners and one for private and housing association tenants. The guides cost 50p each.

family income supplement

FIS is a weekly cash payment for a family on low wages with one or more dependent children under 16 (or still at school and under 19). Unlike supplementary benefit where you are not eligible if you work more than a certain number of hours a week, FIS is paid only if you work at least so-many hours each week. When a couple have separated, either parent can claim, provided she or he works not less than 24 hours a week and the children are living with her or him.

DHSS leaflet FIS 1 includes a claim form and gives details of conditions and rates.

The amount of the supplement is one-half of the difference between the parent's gross income and the appropriate FIS level for the size of the family. Certain items of income are disregarded, such as child benefit, gifts from relatives, payments in kind. A lump sum awarded as part of financial provision on marriage breakdown would be disregarded, but interest from savings or capital is taken into account when assessing entitlement to FIS.

Family income supplement is tax-free. Once the parent is eligible, the payment is made for a whole year, even if financial circumstances change. This may mean that an increase in the mother's income through maintenance payments during the currency of the FIS award would not affect the amount of FIS being paid to her. And it may be possible for the registrar to give the husband a few months' breathing space by ordering lower maintenance payments until just before the current FIS assessment runs out and, in the order, provide for an increase at that time. The order would be, for example, for £8 per month for 5 months and £30 per month thereafter.

FIS or SB?

It is possible to be a full-time worker for FIS purposes (24 hours a week if a single parent) and part-time for supplementary benefit purposes (less than 30 hours a week).

Single parents who work between 24 and 30 hours a week face a tricky calculation: are they better off claiming FIS or SB? You can go to a citizens advice bureau and ask for help with working out the answer in your particular circumstances.

child benefit

Where a married couple are living together, child benefit is normally paid to the wife. But if the couple separate or divorce, child benefit will be paid to the parent (either or both) with whom the children are living.

You should report your separation or divorce to your local social security office if you are getting child benefit, or if you have not been getting it yet but now have one or more of your children living with you. The claim form is CH2.

one-parent benefit

One-parent benefit is paid to a separated or divorced parent who is getting child benefit. The amount is not increased if there are more children than just one. (More information and a claim form are in leaflet CH11.)

You can claim after you have been living apart from your spouse for 13 weeks, or from the date of your divorce or legal separation if this is sooner than the 13 weeks. But it is not paid if you start living with someone as husband and wife.

Both child benefit and one-parent benefit are counted in when supplementary benefit entitlement is calculated.

Orders the divorce court can make

The court can make more or less any order affecting financial interests that is appropriate.

for periodical payments

An order for periodical payments is a long-term order. It can be made any time after the decree nisi, but does not come into force until the decree absolute. (An order for maintenance pending suit can cover the period from petition to decree absolute.) The order may be expressed as £xx per week/month/year, as the case may be, to be paid to the ex-spouse and/or the children.

secured payments

The court has power to order that the payments be 'secured' by a capital asset that the paying party possesses. A secured order is rare and is only relevant where there is a lot of available capital. It should not be contemplated without legal advice. A secured order can last for the life of the recipient because it survives the death of the payer; no other maintenance order does so.

maintenance for a limited period

Sometimes the court makes an order that, for example, the husband pays his wife £xxxx per annum for the next two years and that thereafter the order ceases. At present, the wife's right to claim further maintenance is not dismissed without her consent. The Matrimonial and Family Proceedings Bill when in force will empower the courts to dismiss outright an application for maintenance.

This limited maintenance, sometimes called 'term maintenance', is usually only ordered where both husband and wife are relatively young, there are no children, the marriage is relatively short and all that is needed is maintenance for a brief period to enable the other person, usually the wife, to find her feet.

for adjustment of property

The divorce court has wide powers to deal with the couple's property. 'Property' is used for any asset, such as a car or items of furniture, not just an owner-occupied matrimonial home and not just assets acquired in the course of the marriage.

A variety of orders can be made re-distributing the assets and the matrimonial home.

The court can
★ order the transfer of possessions from single or joint ownership to one or other of the spouses
★ order the home to be sold and the proceeds of sale to be divided in such proportions as the court thinks appropriate; the sale can be ordered to be postponed
★ give one party the right to stay on in the matrimonial home until a certain date or event (usually the parent who has custody of the children or a wife who has inadequate resources of her own), the house then to be sold and the proceeds divided
★ transfer ownership of the home outright from one spouse to the other
★ transfer a tenancy from one spouse to the other.

for a lump sum

This is precisely what it says: an order that one person pays an amount of cash to the other. A lump sum order may be made if one of the couple has large assets that are readily realisable in cash, such as stocks and shares.

The court sometimes makes a lump sum order when one spouse is to buy out the other's interest in the former matrimonial home.

Lump sum

A lump sum is a once-and-for-all payment which cannot be varied or asked for a second time.

It can be ordered to compensate the wife for money she had to spend after the breakdown of the marriage on maintaining herself and the children, paying off family debts or keeping up mortgage repayments, paying rates, or similar expenditure. Often a lump sum order is the only way of reimbursing the wife for payments she has made prior to the petition because even a maintenance pending suit order from the divorce court cannot be backdated to any time earlier than the filing of the petition. In her application, the wife should give details of payments she made which should have been borne by the husband, so that the court can make an order for the appropriate total sum.

A lump sum payment may be ordered, possibly in conjunction with a property adjustment order, so as to share out fairly the total assets of husband and wife. The potential income from the capital transferred is taken into account by the court when ordering an amount of maintenance. A wealthy wife may be ordered to pay a lump sum to the husband, perhaps to enable him to buy a house.

The court can order the lump sum payment to be made by instalments. It cannot order the money to be raised by borrowing. It can, however, make a lump sum order which the husband has not got the present means to pay, if it is satisfied that the husband has the ability to raise a loan where the sum can be borrowed without necessitating a sale that would be financially crippling to him (for example, selling a business or agricultural land).

A lump sum can be awarded to either party in addition to or instead of maintenance payments.

instead of maintenance

Where the husband has substantial capital available, a lump sum payment to the wife can take the place of maintenance for her, wholly or partially. A lump sum payment helps to remove the bitterness which periodical payments can cause: once the capital payment is made, the parties can regard the book as closed.

From the husband's point of view, one lump sum payment instead of making periodical payments to his former wife may well be attractive. However, if she marries again only a few months after receiving a substantial lump sum in lieu of maintenance, the ex-husband would have no redress unless the wife at the time of the order knew of her impending marriage and did not disclose it, in which case the husband might be able to appeal.

A lump sum payment in lieu of periodical payments is not always satisfactory for the recipient. Periodical payments tend to bear a fairly direct relationship to the payer's earnings and the order can be taken to the court from time to time for review as and when circumstances change – whereas a lump sum order cannot be added to.

for children

A lump sum order can also be made in favour of children; trustees would have to be appointed during the children's minority (that is, until they reach the age of 18).

Such an order could be applied for in circumstances where the father might have expended capital for the children if the marriage had not broken down – for example, for school fees. Any income such a lump sum could produce would be taken into account when the court assesses the amount of maintenance to be paid for the children.

Lump sum payments to children can involve capital transfer tax problems and advice should be taken about this.

side-effects of a lump sum

If the recipient of a lump sum is legally aided, a lump sum of over £2,500 may be reduced by the legal aid fund's statutory charge.

And if the lump sum brings the recipient's total capital above the limit for getting legal aid, the legal aid certificate may be withdrawn even if there are other legal matters still needing a solicitor, so that the further work remaining to be done by the solicitor will have to be paid by the client personally.

Similarly, a lump sum payment may put the recipient outside supplementary benefit limits.

deliberately disposing of assets

If the wife fears or suspects that the husband, in order to avoid making proper financial provision for her or the children, is getting rid of assets (possibly to a woman with whom he is living, or into a bank account elsewhere) or is deliberately spending capital by living extravagantly, she should immediately apply to the divorce court for an order preventing her husband from disposing of assets or for an order setting aside any disposal which has taken place. In support of her application, she would have to provide an affidavit giving all the relevant facts. (Husbands also can, and do, make such an application.)

The court will assume that the proposed or actual disposition was carried out with the intention of preventing the wife or children obtaining payment where such a disposition has taken place within the three years prior to the application, or is about to take place – unless the husband can prove the contrary.

A disposition – for instance, the sale of a house – will not be set aside, however, if the buyer acted in good faith, paid the full value and was unaware of the seller's intentions. But if the property was sold for less than the true value, the judge may consider this an indication of collusion between husband and buyer, and may be able to set the sale aside.

Agreements

There is nothing to prevent you coming to whatever agreement over money that you like and both going your separate ways without involving the court at all. But if there is money and property to divide, it is generally better to have an agreement that you have come to embodied in a court order. There are tax advantages in having maintenance payments in the form of a court order, especially where you are paying money for your children. Also, a court order is generally easier to enforce or to get changed if there is later disagreement.

voluntary agreements

A husband and wife can come to an agreement between themselves about their financial and property arrangements when divorcing.

The advantages of a voluntary agreement are privacy (contentious matters are not aired before officials) and that no legal evidence (such as ground for divorce or neglect to maintain) is needed.

Apart from any agreement affecting the house, an agreement need not be recorded in writing to be binding (but it is better that it should be). Such an agreement constitutes a contract, so that if it were broken, the case could be taken to court and you could sue for breach of contract to enforce it. However, in circumstances where agreement was reached by duress or by one of the spouses exercising undue influence on the other, the contract may not be upheld by the court.

An informal arrangement means that the payee does not have to declare the income to the Inland Revenue, but the payer gets no tax relief on the payments. If, however, a statement of the terms has been signed by both husband and wife and a copy of the agreement has been sent to the Inland Revenue, and the Inland Revenue accepts that the terms of the agreement are clear enough to be enforceable by the courts, the payer will be entitled to set the payments off against his tax. But the recipient will be liable to tax on the agreed payments made.

drawbacks

There is no overall tax advantage in making voluntary payments for children. (Only where there is a court order is it possible to take advantage of the children's personal tax allowances.)

If a wife later wants to obtain a mortgage in her own name, it will be necessary to convince the building society that she has sufficient income to pay the interest – a court order will be more valuable than evidence of an amount paid voluntarily.

changes to the agreement

It is generally advisable to have a solicitor's help in drawing up an agreement or an application to the court for any order dealing with financial provision or property. The solicitor will require all the information and documentation about circumstances, resources and commitments. The solicitor may refuse to accept that the agreement that the clients have come to is satisfactory for both of them, and may disturb the goodwill they have established with each other. He may point out that the agreement is not the best that could be achieved for you. He is acting in accordance with his duty to you, but you may reject that advice if you wish.

The couple can at any time vary the agreement if they both want to – possibly making an endorsement on the original agreement. If agreement to alter it cannot be reached, either is entitled to apply to the court for an order on the proposed different terms. No agreement can prevent the court, at the request of one of the parties, from reviewing the agreement and changing its terms.

consent order

Terms agreed by the couple can be submitted to the court and the registrar asked to make an order 'by consent'. This can be done when applying for directions for trial under the special procedure for divorce or at decree nisi stage.

An application for a consent order should give details of the agreed terms and be signed by both husband and wife indicating their consents.

Before finalising an agreement, you should be sure that the other person has made a full disclosure of his or her income from all sources and any factors likely to affect the agreement, such as remarriage. Registrars' practice varies, but most require an agreed statement of both parties' means and liabilities; some registrars require to be supplied with a note of the tax implications of the orders they are asked to make.

Provided the registrar has sufficient information to be satisfied that the proposed terms are reasonable, he will accept the agreement and issue a formal consent order without either party having to come before him. If the agreement is put forward by solicitors on each side, the registrar may approve it without an attendance or further evidence, relying on the solicitors having investigated and advised.

The registrar is, however, not bound to make an order in the agreed terms. He may require the couple to come and explain how they came to agree on the proposed arrangements and the particular figures, especially where there are children and, on the information provided, the suggested maintenance seems low. Also, if the maintenance figure is low and there seems to be some possibility of pressure, he may ask the couple for affidavits of means.

after a consent order

The words 'liberty to apply' are usually written into the wording of a consent order. The effect of this is to allow either party to go back to the court, should they have any problems with the implementation of the order.

Another common provision is that where property is made over wholly or substantially to one party, the order states that the other agrees that all other claims that could be made against the transferor of the property be formally dismissed. Without this provision, the receiving party could resurrect the other claims (although it is unlikely that the court would entertain such a claim sympathetically). Similarly, the agreement can stipulate that the payee shall not claim on the payer's estate if he or she dies before the recipient.

A consent order can be set aside on ground of fresh evidence that could not have been known at the time; fundamental mistakes such as wholly erroneous information on which all parties, including the court, relied; fraud (which may include evidence that the other party has no intention of ever abiding by the terms of the order).

in the magistrates' court

If you do not get divorced immediately (perhaps awaiting two years of separation to elapse), you may still want to get an order for the maintenance you have agreed between you, because of the tax advantages. It is simple to have any agreement for maintenance made into a court order at the magistrates' court, provided the court is satisfied that the agreement is reasonable.

Which court to apply to

	divorce county court	magistrates' court
you can apply if:	can show ground for divorce and/or that spouse has failed to maintain	spouse has failed to maintain or behaves 'unreasonably' or has deserted or both have agreed the arrangement
orders can be made for:	maintenance pending suit (m.p.s) mutually agreed arrangements ('consent' order) periodical payments to spouse and/or children property adjustment (to sell or transfer home or other assets) lump sum payment to spouse and/or children variation of existing maintenance order(s) or agreement	interim maintenance (3 months' duration, extendable to 6 months) periodical payments to spouse and/or children lump sum payment to spouse and/or children (up to £500 each) mutually agreed arrangements
application can be made:	once divorce petition filed at court	at any time during marriage
order lasts until:	death of recipient death of payer (unless payments 'secured') remarriage of recipient child becomes 17 (unless order specifically extended to age of 18, or older for educational or other special reasons) variation or discharge granted expiry of term fixed in order	equivalent divorce court order made parties resume living together for more than 6 months death of recipient or payer child becomes 17 (unless order specifically extended to age of 18, or older for educational or other special reasons) variation or discharge granted

The home before a divorce

The Matrimonial Homes Act gives a spouse who is not the legal owner of the matrimonial home certain rights of occupation:

- the right not to be evicted without a court order if he or she is in occupation
- the right (if the court thinks fit) to return to the home if he or she has left it.

The same rights apply if the home is rented.

These are short-term rights of occupation while the marriage is still in being. The long-term decisions about the rights to live in the home, or to get a share of the proceeds if sold, will have to be made as part of the divorce settlement.

getting an injunction

The realities of life are that one spouse may try to force the other to leave, by violent means or other pressure. Where there is actual or feared violence, or behaviour that may cause harm, a court order can be obtained against the threatening spouse, requiring him or her to leave, or not return to the home, or to confine himself or herself to a defined part of the home, or not to assault, molest or in any way interfere with the other spouse and/or children.

These two forms of injunction are commonly referred to as an 'ouster' injunction and a 'non-molestation' injunction. In the magistrates' court, it is possible to get similar protection by an exclusion order or a protection order.

The application for an injunction can be made to the appropriate county court or magistrates' court, whether or not divorce proceedings have started or are envisaged. Where divorce proceedings have started, 'ouster' proceedings can be brought in the same county court as the one where the divorce is being carried on.

You should get a solicitor's help with an application for an injunction. (The green form scheme allows for a solicitor's advice on applying for an injunction.) Equally, if an injunction is served on you, you should get legal advice.

The cost of obtaining an injunction is likely to be some hundreds of pounds.

Legal aid is available for an injunction and it is possible for an emergency legal aid certificate to be granted immediately.

applying

An application for an injunction has to be supported by an affidavit giving particulars of any children, of the accommodation and alternative accommodation available to each party, and of the conduct complained of, and why an injunction is necessary.

The other spouse should produce an affidavit dealing with the allegations and can suggest solutions, such as alternative accommodation or the possibility of remaining living in the same house.

An emergency application for an injunction can be heard very quickly – usually in a few days or, in a real emergency, straightaway even without written affidavit evidence.

Before making an ouster injunction, the judge will want to be satisfied both that the circumstances warrant such an order and that there is no satisfactory alternative in the light of the spouses' conduct and the accommodation available.

Bear in mind the consequences of seeking and obtaining an ouster injunction in terms of your future relationship: if that is the way your divorce proceedings begin, the prospect of negotiating reasonably and reaching a sensible agreement recedes dramatically.

in the magistrates' court

The magistrates' court can be asked for a personal protection order to restrain a spouse who has threatened violence towards the other spouse and/or children. When it is essential to have protection without delay, an expedited order can be made; most courts will arrange a hearing the same day.

Where actual physical injury has been caused to the other spouse or to a child, or violence threatened or used towards any other person, the magistrates' court can be asked for an exclusion order. This orders the violent spouse to leave the home or, if he or she has already left, not to return.

Where a person is receiving advice under the green form scheme, an application can be made to the legal aid area office for approval of 'assistance by way of representation' (known as ABWOR) which, if granted, covers a solicitor's representing his client in the magistrates' court for an application for an exclusion order or a protection order. This is one of the few circumstances in which a solicitor can appear in court under the green form scheme.

a right of occupation

A spouse who does not legally own the home – that is, whose name is not on the title deeds – has the right, if in occupation, to go on living there and not be evicted or, if not in occupation, has the right, with the permission of the court, to go back and live in the home.

These rights not to turn you out of the home or deny you access are binding only on your spouse. However, by registering your rights (at HM Land Registry if the land is registered or the Land Charges Department if the land is unregistered), you can protect your rights against subsequent buyers or mortgagees.

If you do not register your rights and the home is sold, the buyer or building society may not be bound by them and could turn you out, unless you were living in the home when it was sold or mortgaged and you had not consented to the sale or mortgage taking place.

Rights of occupation (whether registered or not) come to an end on the death of either spouse or when the decree absolute is granted. (So it may be advisable not to apply for the decree until property issues have been settled.) The court may extend the rights of occupation after the end of the marriage if asked to do so.

Although it is possible to register your rights of occupation at any time before the house is actually sold (even after someone has signed a contract to buy it, provided you have not agreed not to register your rights), you should do so as soon as possible because your husband or wife may take steps to sell the home or take out a mortgage on it, without telling you.

Find out, first of all, whether your house has a registered title or not, because there are different ways of registering your rights depending on whether the land is registered or unregistered. An incorrect registration is ineffective.

But it is important that you act quickly. If you are in any doubt, or time is short, apply to register at both places until you have sorted out the position. If you find out that the title is registered at the Land Registry, you should cancel the land charge at the Land Charges Registry.

If the house is mortgaged, you can ask the building society to tell you whether the title to your house is registered.

The Land Registry (Lincoln's Inn Fields, London WC2A 3PH telephone 01-405 3488) can be asked for their explanatory leaflet (no. 9) which lists the counties and districts in England and Wales where there is compulsory registration and includes the addresses of the district land registries for the areas.

The land registry for your area will advise you how to make a search to determine whether the particular address is registered, and will also provide details of the necessary forms and procedure for you to register your right.

registered property

The way of protecting your rights of occupation against third parties if the property is registered is by registering a notice. Land Registry form 99 has to be used. It is available from government bookshops and law stationers shops (not from the Land Registry).

In order to register the notice, it is necessary to know the full names of the registered proprietor and the title number of the property. If the latter is not known, it can be discovered by carrying out a search of the index map at the district land registry. There is no fee for an index map search when it is stated to be for the purpose of the Matrimonial Homes Act. If you can go in person to the appropriate registry, the search and application for registration of the notice can be made there and then. Alternatively, a postal search for the title number can be made, provided the property can be adequately described. Land Registry form 96 should be used for a postal search. This and the application to register the notice can be submitted together (leaving the title number blank for completion by the Land Registry). The fee for registering a notice is £3.

unregistered property

If the title to the property is not registered, a 'class F' land charge should be registered at the Land Charges Department, Burrington Way, Plymouth PL5 3LP. The form to be used, K2, is available from government bookshops and law stationers shops. The information required includes the full name in which the property-owning spouse bought or acquired the property and a description of it. The fee for registration is 50p.

act quickly

The green form scheme allows a solicitor to deal with registration of a land charge or a notice.

All citizens advice bureaux can help with filling in the forms to register a right of occupation and some have a supply of the necessary forms. It may be quicker to go to a CAB than to get an appointment with a solicitor.

the effect of registering a charge or notice

Anyone buying the property or granting a mortgage on it would as a matter of routine check the appropriate registry and discover your notice defending your rights. (Even if a subsequent buyer or mortgagee does not actually search the register or has no knowledge of the registration, the effect of registering a land charge or notice amounts in law to notice of the non-owning spouse's right of occupation.) If he then buys the house or gives the mortgage, he does so subject to your right of occupation and cannot turn you out unless you have agreed to release your rights.

The effect of registration normally ceases once a decree of divorce is made absolute. If the question of the matrimonial home has not been settled by then, the non-owning spouse should ask the court before the decree is made absolute to give permission for the registration of the class F land charge or the notice to be renewed after the decree absolute. An order for renewal of the registration of a notice or charge must also be protected by registration.

Resources and needs

You and your spouse should discuss and, if possible, agree your financial arrangements, rather than dissipate your funds and energy by arguments and protracted litigation. Try to understand that the only money available will have to come from what you each have and it has to be shared between you as fairly as possible. If the proceedings become expensive because you argued over every single point, you will have less, and so will your former spouse. Remember that the law cannot create assets which are not there nor spread money farther than it can go.

a solicitor's help

When going to see a solicitor about the arrangements for the financial terms of your divorce, let the solicitor concentrate on the legal or tax aspects of the wording of orders rather than on disentangling the basic information about your practical affairs. Do not expect the solicitor to work out your milk and gas bills or to go rummaging around in three boxes of papers going back ten years. In order not to waste the solicitor's time and therefore your money, do as much preparation as you can beforehand, so that you can present him or her quickly and concisely with the information that will be needed. Prepare a clear, accurate and complete statement about your financial position and that of your spouse; get together and take with you documents to prove your outgoings.

If you present your lawyer with a list of your assets and liabilities, and a copy of your proposed budget, you will be charged only for the solicitor's time spent reading through the papers and later transferring the facts to the court form. By doing the preparation, you will have saved perhaps one to two hours of the solicitor's time for which he would have charged.

If you do not supply the correct information, you are wasting money. If you do not heed the advice you are given, it may cost money in the future.

information needed for your solicitor or yourself

1 details about your home

★ who lives there – including adult children, lodgers, dependent relatives (if your spouse has left, when that happened)
★ number of bedrooms, living rooms
★ what the rates are (general, sewerage, water)
★ who has been paying which household bills
★ who has done, or paid for, any work on the house

if you own your home

★ what is it worth?
(an approximate estimate)
★ how did you arrange your finances to pay for the house?
★ who put down the deposit?
★ what substantial improvements have been made to the property since purchase (e.g. central heating)? what was the cost and how was it paid for?
★ if there is a mortgage:
(ask the building society for any of these facts if you do not know them)
(a) how much is outstanding?
(b) what are the monthly payments?
(c) when will it be paid off?
(d) if it is an endowment mortgage, when is the policy due to mature and for how much? what are the current surrender and paid-up values? (ask the insurance company)
(e) name, address and account/reference number of the building society, bank or other lender
★ is the house in joint names?
(this is important – if you find that the house is in your spouse's name only, the house could be sold without your agreement or knowledge but you can take steps to prevent this happening provided you or your solicitor act quickly)
★ is the title registered?

if you rent your home

★ is it rented from the council, a housing association, a private landlord?
★ how much rent do you pay? (weekly, monthly, quarterly)
★ is it a regulated tenancy?
★ in whose name is the tenancy? (take along a copy of the tenancy agreement, if you have it)
★ is there a service or maintenance charge? if so, how much?

2. house contents and personal items

★ what are your proposals for dividing the contents of the house – furniture, china, carpets etc – between you and your spouse? (It is relatively rare for there to be an equal split of furniture: in most cases where there are children, the wife needs and gets the bulk.)
★ are there any items of special value (e.g. jewellery or antiques) which you feel are personal to you or to your spouse and not available to be shared? (if so, estimate their value)
★ why do you consider those you claim are yours personally and not joint property?
★ were they paid for out of a joint account or from housekeeping money? or were they presents? if so, from whom?

3. car

★ do you own a car?
   (if so, make, model, year, value)
★ does your spouse own a car?
   (if so, make, model, year, value)
★ will you and/or your spouse need a car in the future?
★ do you or your spouse have the use of a company car?

4. your own employment

If you are self-employed, you may be required to produce recent years' accounts. (A housewife may be surprised to discover that what she earns from e.g. mail order clubs, jewellery parties, may be taken into account.)

★ details of your present employment: name of employer, nature of job, whether full or part-time (if currently not employed, details and dates of last employment and qualifications)
★ normal weekly or monthly earnings (produce P.60 form or a copy: this shows gross earnings, tax, national insurance payments and pension contributions for the previous tax year) and at least the last 4 payslips
★ any fringe benefits, commission or bonuses regularly received
★ expenses of getting to your job and of any clothing and equipment essential for your job
★ cost of child-minding or nursery school for child while you are at work
★ any other relevant information, such as imminent promotion or redundancy

Also provide as many of the above details as possible about your spouse's employment and earnings. (Do not worry about the P.60 form – he/she can be asked to produce it in due course.)

5. pension

★ details of any pension or superannuation scheme to which you belong (occupational or personal plan)
★ does pension scheme entitle widow(er) to benefit? (you will probably lose any benefits as a result of divorce because you become an ex-spouse rather than a widow)

6. other assets and income

Make a list of:
★ any joint accounts you have
★ savings in building society, bank deposit, savings accounts
★ stocks and shares
★ the interest you get from them
★ life insurance policy(ies) owned by yourself or your spouse: how much? when maturing?
★ valuables, such as jewellery, antiques

7. maintenance

★ maintenance payments (if any) made to your former wife and/or to your child/ren

or

★ maintenance payments received from former husband (or wife)

★ any regular provision to/from someone else (if paid under a court order, give reference number or copy of order to solicitor)

8. payments from DHSS

★ what money do you receive from the DHSS? for example,
supplementary benefit
family income supplement
child benefit
retirement pension
invalidity benefit

All this information will have to be included in an 'affidavit of means', as part of your application for financial provision to the divorce court.

You may also be expected to provide information (with figures, as precise as you can) of the necessary expenses of running your home: gas, electricity, telephone, insurance, hire purchase commitments and other regular debts.

Calculating resources and needs

In some marriages, both may know all there is to know about each other's financial affairs because resources have always been pooled and property has been in joint names. But if this is not the case, it is essential to discover exactly what you each have at present and work out what you are likely to need in the future.

The first step is to calculate your assets, liabilities, income and needs.

assets and liabilities

First make a list of all the capital assets that you own and then subtract your liabilities. For example, you need to deduct the amount outstanding on your mortgage from the value of your house. If you are not sure how much your house is now worth, have a look in the local estate agents' windows and advertisements in local newspapers for the prices of similar properties.

The following checklist will help to give you some idea, but there may well be other things on your particular list.

present assets	present liabilities
home	amounts outstanding on mortgage(s)
car(s) and/or	hire purchase or credit agreement
motorcycle, caravan, boat	other debts
savings and investments:	bank overdraft
building society account(s)	bank loan
bank accounts: current, deposit	other loans
National Savings certificates	outstanding balance on credit card
premium bonds	budget account
life insurance policies	....
pension plan	....
stocks and shares	

valuable contents of the home:
  antiques
  pictures
  hifi
  piano
  computer equipment
  silver
  jewellery
  ....
  ....
total assets £......   total liabilities £......

Some of the assets may not be realisable from a practical point of view (or financially foolish at that moment).

It is usually a waste of time counting in as assets the everyday household belongings because they have no tangible resale value. They tend to be more relevant as a 'need' for the person who is moving out and who is therefore likely to have the cost of replacing them.

At this stage, you can begin to discuss realistically how you are going to split the assets: for example, 50/50 or 60/40 or whatever.

Ownership tends to be an irrelevant issue. The basic principle is that marriage as such does not affect the property rights between husband and wife. For example, if on marriage they move into a house owned solely by the husband, the marriage does not affect his ownership; if the wife is left money, the money belongs to her. On marriage breakdown, however, all the money and property become part of the couple's assets, on which each spouse has a claim.

income

Remember to take everything into account:

• net salary or wages from employment, including any overtime (if this is irregular, work out annual amount and then average over a week or month. Most payslips give the cumulative total for taxable pay and the number of the week or month: divide the former by the latter to work out average weekly or monthly pay.)
For someone who is self-employed, calculations should be based on accountants' figures over the last three years.

• casual work, freelance work
• interest on building society or bank accounts
• income from other investments
• pension(s)
• payments from DHSS

current expenditure and future needs

It is generally difficult to think of where your money goes; identifying the types of outlay under three headings may help:

• day-to-day spending
• regular payments
• occasional lump sums

Note how much you spend on each and try to decide which are the essential items.
Your checklist may include:

babysitter
bank charges
books

car: insurance, repairs, servicing,
   tax; petrol, oil;
 AA/RAC subscription
childminder
Christmas
cigarettes
clothes
cosmetics (e.g. soap, shampoo,
   chemists' goods)

dentist
drink (at home, pub, club, bar)
dry cleaning

electricity
entertainments (cinema, concerts,
   theatre, bingo)

fares
fees (professional, school, college)
food
fuel (coal, coke, firewood,
   charcoal)

garden
gas
general household (e.g. lavatory paper, cleaning materials, light bulbs, batteries)
ground rent

hairdresser
help in the home
HP and other credit payments
hobbies
holidays
home decorating and repairs

insurance premiums (car, home, life etc)

launderette/laundry

maintenance or service charge
meals out
medicines, prescriptions
mortgage payments

newspapers, magazines

oil for central heating
outings for children
overdraft interest

paraffin
payments to dependants
pets (food, vet's bills etc)
photography (films, developing)

pocket money for children
presents
private lessons (e.g. music)
private medical insurance

rates
records, cassettes, tapes
rent

savings (regular scheme)
school, nursery, fees
school meals
season ticket(s)
servicing and repairs of household equipment (e.g. washing machine, central heating unit)
shoes and shoe repairs
spectacles
sports (equipment, gate money, subscriptions)
stamps and stationery
subscriptions to associations, charities, clubs, trade union
sweets, chocolates, icecream

telephone
tools
TV licence; repairs or rental

water charges
window cleaning

Your own checklist should be as complete as possible to be of help to you both. The figures against the items should come from receipted accounts, cheque stubs, credit card statements.

If you have no idea of how much you do spend on what, take a notebook with you every day when you go shopping for, say, two to four weeks, and write everything down. This exercise should be done by both of you, especially if you are already living at different addresses. If your children are old enough to understand, encourage them to note what they spend (it may also make them feel less left out of the future plans which each parent is making).

When the immediate financial picture is as complete as you can make it, you can try to estimate how much you will each need in the future.

Not all the items will be doubled when you split up: some will be halved, some reduced, some will stay the same and may be paid for by either of you. For instance, electricity will be paid twice, cigarettes and cosmetics divided, school meals and private lessons unchanged. A probable future spending pattern for each of you should emerge from this.

for the court

Apart from giving you a better idea of what you both have and what money you are likely to need in the next year or so, this information will be needed for the registrar at the divorce court. If you consult a solicitor, by providing this information you can give him or her a better idea of your financial situation, for the negotiations.

However wide the court's powers may appear to be, the scope is usually limited by the resources available. The court will try to ensure that the financial loss that you are both suffering is evenly spread. Your standards of living are likely to be reduced, so avoid reducing them further by running up large legal fees because of protracted arguments.

How the court decides

In divorce proceedings, the court is governed by a number of statutory guidelines set out in section 25 of the Matrimonial Causes Act 1973. The Matrimonial and Family Proceedings Bill awaiting royal assent in July 1984 will make the welfare of the children the predominant consideration. The new Bill also directs the court to consider whether it would be appropriate to terminate the financial obligations of each of the couple towards the other after the divorce and when it would be fair and reasonable to do so.

The court is required to have regard to income, earning capacity and potential earning capacity, property and other financial resources and

★ your financial needs, obligations and responsibilities at present and in the foreseeable future
★ your ages
★ the length of the marriage
★ the standard of living of the family before the breakdown
★ any mental or physical disability
★ any contributions made by either of you to the family's welfare (whether in cash or in kind)
★ in some circumstances, your conduct
★ the value of any future benefits which either of you has lost the chance of acquiring (e.g. pension rights) as a result of the divorce.

Guidelines

There is no such thing as set rates for maintenance to be paid to a spouse. (Maintenance for children is considered separately.)

The way the courts apply their guidelines is – and must be – flexible to meet particular needs. What the court can do in any case is largely limited by the resources available to the particular couple.

one-third starting point

The court will usually start by adding together both parties' incomes and take as a starting point for maintenance whatever amount is required to bring the applicant's pre-tax income up to one-third of the joint incomes.

The basis of the calculations are the earnings of both partners before tax but after deducting national insurance contributions, any pension contributions and expenses of travelling to work. Earnings include all bonuses, commission, overtime payments, not just basic flat rates, and any income from part-time work; also income from investments. Capital sums, such as savings, are relevant if the capital may be better invested where it would yield a higher return and provide more income.

The court takes into account the impact of tax and any other relevant factors to produce a 'net effect' – that is, what income you would each be left with if the one-third formula were applied.

other factors

The one-third is only a rule of thumb used as a starting point. Other factors may require it to be varied upwards or downwards, depending upon the parties' means.

can the wife be expected to go out to work?

A young woman with no children would be expected to go out to work.

If there are young children at home, the court would not expect the mother to go out to work. However, a mother with a young family who has been going out to work before the break-up of the marriage may be expected to go on earning if practicable. (But not where her ability to work before the break-up depended on the husband's helping to look after the children.)

If the children are grown up and she has not worked for many years, there may simply not be suitable available employment. Because of the present employment situation, it may well be that a woman who has not been working will be unable to get a job anyway.

A wife who has never had a job may think why should she work now (especially if she believes that her ex-husband will then have more money to keep himself and his new companion). If the husband thinks that the wife is deliberately refusing work, it is no good his just saying this without being able to come up with specific information as to jobs which are available and which she has the capability to do.

Where the wife has worked before, it will be hard for her to justify that she need not do so now.

A father who is caring for young children is in the same position as a mother in that he is not to be expected to take on a job. There is usually no difference between father and mother in this respect, except that more frequently the husband is able to earn more and this may make it more realistic for him to go to work, getting in a housekeeper or childminder.

Husband or wife being capable of earning more would not usually be regarded as relevant, unless he or she is deliberately depressing his or her earnings in order to influence the maintenance claim. In such a case, the court will make orders based on what he or she should be able to earn. (The new Bill contains provision for the court to take into account steps which it would be reasonable to expect a party to take to increase earning capacity.)

length of the marriage

If it is a short marriage and there are no children, the court may be inclined not to order maintenance, or perhaps for a limited period only. A short marriage between a young couple who are both working or able to do so is likely to be treated very differently from a short marriage between two people in, say, their mid-fifties where the woman had given up secure accommodation to come and live with the husband.

Whether a period of time living together before marriage is taken into account is at the court's discretion. It is likely to be so if children were born during that period, or if one party had made a substantial financial contribution to the shared home before marriage.

pension rights

One factor the court has to consider is the possible loss by a divorced woman (or, less frequently, a man) of a right to a widow's pension under an occupational pension scheme of which the husband is a contributing member.

The trustees of a pension scheme have to abide by the rules of the scheme. These may allow discretion on the part of the trustees to decide who should get what. The rules may stipulate paying the widow's (or widower's) pension to the legal widow (or widower), and if there is no legal wife, a pension can be paid for the benefit of an orphan of the marriage or any adult dependant. A pension cannot normally be divided between a legal wife and an ex-wife. An orphan's right to a pension would not be lost on divorce, although it would be divided between the orphans of the first and any subsequent marriage.

Although an ex-wife cannot claim any share of a widow's pension, she could try to claim a dependant's benefit or (perhaps part of) the scheme's lump sum benefit. Occupational pension schemes normally include a lump sum death benefit of up to four times' a member's pay on his death before retirement. The trustees would normally take into account the member's wishes in the 'expression of wish' form which he will have completed when he joined the scheme. (A scheme member can at any time alter his nomination of whom he wishes to get the lump sum.) After divorce, on the death of the husband the trustees may be able to use their discretion where appropriate to divide the lump sum between the ex-wife and any current legal wife or cohabitant.

Many pension schemes provide that on the death of a member after retirement, the widow will be entitled to perhaps one half of the pension prospectively due to be received by her late husband. Under the majority of pension schemes, a divorced former spouse is not likely to be eligible.

Under some pension schemes, a member may be able (though cannot be forced) to give up part of his own pension at retirement to provide in return a pension for his ex-spouse after his death.

loss of pension rights

The court can try to have the wife compensated for loss of what her pension entitlement would be. It cannot order the husband to take out life insurance or an annuity, but it can order the husband to provide capital by way of a lump sum to enable her to buy a deferred annuity for that amount, to start at his death or at retirement age and to continue until her death. (But this may be prohibitively expensive.)

An alternative solution is to increase the wife's share in the matrimonial home by way of compensating her for the loss of pension rights.

Where the divorce is based on separation (especially when it is not one by consent) and the court is asked to consider what the respondent's financial position will be after divorce, the court may refuse to allow the decree to be made absolute unless and until a satisfactory insurance policy has been taken out to be vested in the wife.

new companion

If either or both of you have formed a new relationship, this may make the break-up of your marriage less financially damaging. The fact that the other is moving out to live with somebody else, although emotionally hurtful, may be the best thing that could happen as far as accommodation costs are concerned. It reduces the biggest financial strain of all – two sets of accommodation costs from one income.

Where the ex-spouse's living expenses and accommodation costs have been substantially reduced because of a new partner's contribution, there is more of the ex-spouses' money to go around and be shared out.

Where a spouse has taken on new liabilities to a new wife or husband or cohabitant, the court takes those liabilities into account when considering the maintenance order, while trying not to reduce the ex-spouse's standard of living to below that of the new spouse.

Basically, the new spouse cannot be required to contribute towards support for the previous spouse and family – but her or his means are taken into account in deciding the paying ex-spouse's liabilities. The court would look at the new partner's capacity to contribute towards their joint expenses. For example, if she pays half the rent or mortgage, the payer could not successfully argue that he should pay less maintenance to his ex-wife because he has a liability to pay the whole rent or mortgage for his new home.

The court does not require to know what a new wife or cohabitant earns, but will want to know the extent to which she or he relieves the ex-spouse from having to provide for her – and also for himself.

In order to be satisfied that the full picture of contribution has been revealed, the new partner's means usually come under review of the court. He or she cannot be forced to produce an affidavit of means but can be summonsed to court and be questioned as to his or her means – unless the court accepts that it would be oppressive to do so.

'conduct'

Under the Matrimonial Causes Act 1973, the divorce court has been required to take the past conduct of each of the partners into account 'so far as it is just to do so'. In the majority of cases, it does not matter who petitions for the decree or whose conduct was the final cause of the break-up of the marriage. Conduct has been interpreted by the courts as conduct which is 'gross and obvious' or 'really serious' or such that it would 'offend one's sense of justice not to take it into account'.

The Matrimonial and Family Proceedings Bill proposes that the court shall have regard to 'the conduct of each of the parties, if that conduct is such that it would in the opinion of the court be inequitable to disregard it'.

The account taken of conduct may, with all the other circumstances, depend on the stage that the marriage has reached, and whether there are children. For example, if one party walked out on the other after only a short period of marriage, little or no maintenance may be ordered but this may be due as much to the fact that the marriage was very short-lived and without children as to 'conduct'.

With a marriage in its middle stage and with children, a wife's 'conduct' is unlikely to have much influence on the financial settlement if to penalise her would mean penalising the children.

Although the applicant's conduct may be put forward as an argument for lower maintenance, the paying spouse's conduct can rarely be argued as a ground for increasing it, unless that spouse had done something (such as a serious criminal assault) that has affected the other's ability to earn a living.

calculation for one-third starting point

Husband	£	£
gross monthly pay		xxx
less:		
national insurance	xx	
pension contribution		
(if compulsory)	xx	
travel to work	xx	xxx
		(A)

Wife		
gross monthly pay		xxx
child benefit		xx
less:		
national insurance	xx	
pension contribution		
(if compulsory)	xx	
childminder	xx	
travel to work	xx	xxx
		(B)

total combined income (A + B)	
divided by 3	xxx
less (B)	xxx

starting point for order
would be:

$$\frac{A + B}{3} - B = £xx$$

registrar's decision

The registrar has to consider what the net effect on husband and wife will be if he makes an order with the one-third formula as the starting point. This means comparing the available income of each of them with their basic outgoings.

'net effect' calculations

Husband	£	Wife	£
gross income:		gross income:	
earnings		earnings	
any other income		any other income	
		child benefit	
		payments from husband	
		children's periodical payments	
less:		*less:*	
tax		tax	
national insurance contributions		national insurance contributions	
pension contributions		pension contributions	
periodical payments to wife		travel to work	
periodical payments to children			
travel to work			
Available income	£	Available income	£

These figures compared with the forecast of your needs may show that one or both of you have got nowhere near enough to meet your projected expenses. Looking at your incomes, needs and available capital (if any), a decision must be reached on how things can be arranged to come up with a more realistic figure. In many cases, it will just have to be accepted that both sides are going to be very hard up, at least for a while.

orders for the children

In making financial orders for children, the court will have regard to the child's financial needs, earning capacity and income and also the manner in which the parents had planned for him or her to be educated or trained.

The court has power to make orders in respect of any 'child of the family'. This is defined as not only a child of both of you (which includes an adopted child) but also any other child whom you have treated as a child of your family (except foster-children).

You could be ordered to make payments for your spouse's children from a former marriage or relationship, provided you had treated them as your children. This liability to maintain is, however, mitigated by the fact that the court is required to consider the liability of any other person to maintain them (for example, their natural parent) and whether, when treating them as your children, you thought they were your own and now you find that they were the result of an adulterous relationship of which you were unaware.

Orders in favour of children requested in the petition can be any of the ones that can be made for a wife or husband. In practice, it is very unusual for the court to do other than order periodical payments for a child. There may be a separate, earlier hearing to order maintenance for the children, before the main financial hearing.

An order for payments to children comes into effect as soon as it is made, even if this is before the decree. Unless the court otherwise provides, an order will not continue beyond the child's 17th birthday (i.e. the one following compulsory school leaving age). But the court has power to make an order to remain in force up to the child's 18th birthday while the child is in full-time education or for longer if there are other special circumstances – for example, disability.

There are no universally accepted guidelines about the financial needs of children: different registrars use different figures. The lowest common denominators are the DHSS allowances for calculating supplementary benefit, which are at present:

child under 11	£ 9.15 per week
child aged 11–15	£13.70 per week
child of 16 or 17	£16.50 per week

A registrar may use these as a guide, multiplied according to the husband's income. For example, if the husband's weekly income is

below £100 – use social security rate
below £125 – use $1\frac{1}{4}$ × social security rate
below £150 – use $1\frac{1}{2}$ × social security rate
below £175 – use $1\frac{3}{4}$ × social security rate
above £175 – use 2 × social security rate

(deducting child benefit which the wife is getting).

In most cases, however, the significant factor is not so much the husband's income as the number of children.

Some registrars will work on the foster parent allowance being paid by the local authority as a more realistic assessment of the cost of maintaining children. In 1984, foster parent basic rates (exclusive of holiday and birthday allowances) recommended by the National Foster Care Association are:

child aged	0–4	£23.87 per week
	5–7	£27.79 per week
	8–10	£30.45 per week
	11–12	£33.11 per week
	13–15	£35.77 per week
	16–18	£47.67 per week

(for London, the recommended rate is 13% higher).

Foster parents are not entitled to child benefit. Registrars take into account the fact that child benefit (at present £6.50 per week per child, plus a payment of £4.05 if a single parent) will be paid to whichever parent has the children living with him or her. Child benefit may be counted in as part of the parent's resources or, more often, it is treated as a contribution towards the cost of maintaining the child or children. The registrar may use either (or neither) of these approaches in his calculations.

Tax and maintenance payments

The way in which the income tax system works for both husband and wife affects the position a good deal.

personal tax allowances

A set amount of every person's annual income is not taxed. Most of these personal allowances change each tax year (which runs from 6 April to 5 April). While a couple are still married, all their income is deemed to be the husband's for tax purposes.

For the tax year 1984/85 the following are the relevant figures.

single person's personal allowance – £2,005

available to single adults and to children, also to anyone separated or divorced and not remarried.

married man's personal allowance – £3,155

available to a married man who is residing with his wife or who is separated and is wholly maintaining her by payments made voluntarily (if paying maintenance to his wife under an enforceable agreement or court order, he gets the single person's allowance).

He continues to get this allowance for the remainder of the tax year in which he separates or gets divorced. If he marries again, he gets this allowance on the basis of his second marriage.

wife's earned income allowance – £2,005 or amount of earned income whichever is lower

available only to a married man whose wife has an income from employment or self-employment.

lone parent's additional personal allowance (APA) – £1,150

can be claimed by a mother or a father, whether separated or divorced, if she or he is eligible for the single person's allowance and has a 'qualifying' child living with him or her for the whole or any part of the tax year (ending 5 April).

The definition of a qualifying child is a complicated one. Basically, you need to show two things:

i) that the child was under 16 at the start of the current tax year. You may, however, still claim for children who are between 16 and 18, if they are receiving full-time instruction at a university, college, school or other educational establishment, or undergoing training for a trade or vocation for the minimum of a two-year period

and

ii) that you are the natural parent or step parent or have adopted the child. If the child is not yours, you may still qualify if you have maintained the child for the whole or part of the current tax year at your own expense, provided he was under 18 at the start of the tax year in which he was adopted.

This allowance is the same whether there is just one child, or any number of children. If the child lives partly with the father and partly with the mother in any one year, the allowance is divided proportionately. Where there are several children, and some live with one parent, some with the other, both parents can claim the full additional personal allowance.

A father will not get the additional personal allowance during a tax year in which he is still getting the married man's allowance.

Details of all personal allowances are given in Inland Revenue leaflet IR22; leaflet IR29 deals with income tax and one-parent families and IR30 with separation and divorce.

income tax

Income tax is payable on the income remaining after taking off personal allowances and deducting certain payments, such as occupational pension contributions, maintenance payments made under a court order. How much tax is payable depends on the amount of taxable income.

current rates of income tax (1984/85 tax year)

	£	£		%
on taxable income of		0 – 15,400	basic rate	30
plus on taxable income of		15,401 – 18,200	higher rate	40
		18,201 – 23,100		45
		23,101 – 30,600		50
		30,601 – 38,100		55
	above	38,100		60

The above rates apply both to income from all sources and to maintenance received under an enforceable agreement or under a court order. If maintenance is 'voluntary', the person who receives it is not liable to tax on it at all.

on break-up of a marriage

When you are splitting up or when you are getting divorced, it is essential that you arrange maintenance payments in such a way as to minimise tax as much as possible. Start by looking at the position when you were still living together.

example

Harry (H) and Wendy (W) in the early stages of their marriage are both working.

		£
total income:	Harry	8,000
	Wendy	7,000
		15,000

	£	£
less: married man's personal tax allowance	3,155	
wife's earned income allowance	2,005	
		5,160
taxable income		9,840

tax due at 30% on £9,840 = £2,952

This will be collected under the PAYE system from both Harry and Wendy's earnings: £1,476 from Harry and £1,476 from Wendy.

Harry and Wendy thus have about £10,700 to live off after they have paid a further £1,300 or so in national insurance contributions.

In November 1984, their marriage having broken down, they separate. In order to calculate tax liability in these circumstances, Wendy's income has to be apportioned into what she earned in the months of the tax year prior to separation and what she has earned afterwards. This is because in the year of the separation

• Harry is entitled to his married man's allowance for the whole of the tax year and for wife's earned income relief on money earned by Wendy in the 7 months of the tax year before the separation

• Wendy is entitled to the single person's allowance in full to set against income she earned in the remaining 5 months of the tax year after the separation.

H's position

		£
total income:	H	8,000
	$W \left(7,000 \times \dfrac{7}{12} \right)$	4,083
		12,083
less: married man's personal tax allowance	3,155	
W's earned income allowance $\left(2,005 \times \dfrac{7}{12} \right)$	1,170	
		4,325
taxable income		7,758

H pays tax at 30% on £7,758 = £2,327

W's position

total income: $7,000 \times \dfrac{5}{12}$ 2,917

less: single person's tax allowance   2,005

taxable income   912

W pays tax at 30% on £912 = £274

In the tax year of separation, Harry and Wendy pay £351 less tax between them than if they had remained together. This is because Wendy has the single person's allowance for the full year to set against her income after separation.

It probably makes sense, all things being equal, not to separate too late in the tax year. If, for example, Harry and Wendy had separated a month before the end of the tax year, her taxable income after separation would have been only £583 (£7,000 $\times$ $^1/_{12}$). Therefore, the full advantage of her single person's allowance would have been lost as she could have earned a further £1,421 tax free in the year of separation.

In the following years, Harry and Wendy would be taxed like any two single people.

action to take

Wendy must notify her tax office as soon as the separation is going to be permanent, otherwise she will end up paying too much tax. Assuming that she is taxed on a PAYE basis, her notice of coding for the year will have taken into account wife's earned income allowance. She must get her coding altered as soon as possible, or alternatively has to make a tax repayment claim at the end of the year.

one spouse paying maintenance to the other

Instead of Wendy being in work when they split up, she had decided to give up work when married and therefore the only one with income is Harry.

if voluntary payment

In this situation where there are no children, it is unlikely that the court will order maintenance but Harry decides he wants to pay her £2,500 per annum voluntarily. Where maintenance is paid voluntarily rather than under a court order or under an enforceable agreement, it remains the payer's income for tax purposes.

H's position

	£
total income	8,000
less: single person's tax allowance	2,005
taxable income	5,995

H pays tax at 30% on £5,995 = £1,799
Harry has (£8,000 − £1,799 − £2,500) = £3,701
Wendy receives £2,500 tax free.

Harry, therefore, has to find £2,500 out of his income after he has paid tax whereas Wendy has no tax burden at all. He is left with less than half his gross income.

if maintenance order

If H pays W either under an enforceable maintenance agreement or subject to a court order

● the £2,500 p.a. ceases to be counted as Harry's income for tax purposes

● the £2,500 now becomes Wendy's income for tax purposes

● the tax is 'collected' for the Inland Revenue by Harry who deducts tax at 30% from the payments that he makes to Wendy. In other words, the maintenance has the tax taken off before it ever reaches Wendy's hands. This can cause serious cash-flow problems for her.

H's position

		£
total income		8,000
less: single person's tax allowance	2,005	
maintenance paid to W	2,500	
		4,505
taxable income		3,495

H pays tax

on own income at 30% on £3,495	1,049
on behalf of Wendy's maintenance at 30% on £2,500	750
	1,799

Harry has (£8,000 − £1,799 − £1,750) = £4,451

Harry pays only £1,750 to Wendy and the Inland Revenue gets the tax on Wendy's maintenance from him during the year through his PAYE.

(If the person deducting the tax is on schedule E – which people working for an employer normally are – his PAYE code number will remain unaltered. If, on the other hand, he is self-employed, he would have to include details of the retained tax in his tax return and the Revenue will raise a separate assessment under schedule D (iii).)

W's position

The £2,500 maintenance is now subject to tax in her hands as follows:

	£
total income: maintenance from H	2,500
less: single person's tax allowance	2,005
taxable income	495

Wendy is liable for tax at 30% on £495 = £149

But Harry has deducted £750 tax over the year when paying her. She has therefore suffered too much tax and must reclaim the tax overpaid (£750 − £149 = £601) from the Inland Revenue.

	£
Wendy has: from Harry	1,750
from the Inland Revenue	601
	2,351

Harry and Wendy between them end up paying £601 *less* tax than they did in the previous example (when he paid her voluntarily). The reason for this is that Wendy's single person's allowance has been utilised, whereas in the previous example it was wasted.

The only problem is that Harry does much better out of this than Wendy: he has an extra £750 per annum, after paying tax and maintenance. She, on the other hand, is £149 worse off. And, in addition, her cash-flow situation is infinitely worse. During the year she receives only £1,750 from Harry and is then left to claim the balance from the Inland Revenue.

action to take

Harry has to supply an R185 form ('certificate of deduction of tax') with each payment. Wendy has to forward these to her tax office with her own claim form R249 (for monthly or quarterly claims) or R40 (for claiming at the end of the financial year) in order to get back the balance from the Inland Revenue. She may not get the money due to her until some considerable time afterwards. And if H fails to produce form R185, this causes extra problems with recovery of tax.

Most tax inspectors deal with tax repayment claims quarterly, some are prepared to do so monthly, so get in touch with your tax inspector as soon as possible and ask what will happen in your case. Some tax offices will not consider a tax repayment claim until the tax return has been filed, so make sure that you complete your tax return promptly.

Cash-flow is a problem mainly during the first months of payments, because subsequently there will be the booster of the tax refund from the previous period. This could be seen as a form of compulsory saving, but a disadvantageous one (particularly if inflation is high).

changing from voluntary payments

A woman may well be getting substantially less in hand when her husband switches over from voluntary maintenance to paying maintenance under a court order, leaving her with the responsibility of making a tax repayment claim. On the other hand, a husband may not realise that if he goes on paying under a court order the same amount that he was paying voluntarily, he is going to have more cash in hand to the extent of 30% of whatever order he is paying.

It is important to work out the tax effect of an order, particularly when it involves a switch from voluntary payments to payments under an order for the first time. For example, H could raise the amount by 43% when switching to a court order, and this would leave W in exactly the same net position as before. A recipient would also be in exactly the same net position if she had other income which swallowed up her tax allowance, but if, as in Wendy's case, she has no other income, she would gain because her single person's allowance would be utilised.

Where the amount of the order is around £1,800 it may be better for the ordered payment to be reduced slightly to make it come within the statutory provisions for 'small maintenance payments'. Small maintenance limits are important unless the wife can afford to wait to get tax repayment and can be certain the husband will provide tax deduction certificates.

'Small maintenance payments'

Where maintenance payable to a spouse under a court order does not exceed £33 per week or £143 per month, the order is treated as a 'small maintenance payment'. Payments made by a voluntary arrangement cannot be treated as small maintenance payments.

The amount of tax which is payable does not alter, only its method of collection:

- the payer does not deduct tax at source but makes each payment gross
- the payer's own PAYE code number will be altered, in order to make up for this
- the recipient, instead of having tax deducted at source, fills in a tax return at the end of the year and will then be assessed for tax. Thus, her cash-flow position is considerably improved.

example

Harry was ordered to pay Wendy £140 a month (which comes to £1,680 a year – but to qualify as a small maintenance payment, the amount ordered must be expressed as payable 'per month' or 'per week', not annually) and Wendy has found a part-time job looking after children which brings her in £30 a week.

H's position

		£
total income		8,000
less: single person's tax allowance	2,005	
maintenance for W	1,680	
		3,685
taxable income		4,315

H pays tax at 30% on £4,315 = £1,295

Harry therefore has (£8,000 − £1,680 − £1,295) = £5,025

In order to ensure that he does not pay too much tax, Harry must tell his tax office as soon as payment under the order begins so that the fact that his taxable income has been reduced can be noted and his notice of coding altered. (The higher the code number, the less tax you pay.) If, for example, payment were to start on 6 April, he would have his coding increased from 200L to 368L. If the order were to start in the middle of the tax year, the code increase would be proportional.

W's position

		£
total income: part-time job	1,560	
maintenance from H	1,680	
		3,240
less: single person's tax allowance		2,005
taxable income		1,235

W is liable to tax at 30% on £1,235 = £371

Wendy therefore has (£3,240 − £371) = £2,869

From a cash-flow point of view, Wendy is better off because within the year she will receive the maintenance in full and does not have to pay the tax on it until later.

If she was paid under PAYE for her part-time employment, Inland Revenue would collect the £371 tax due by altering her notice of coding for the following tax year.

A problem can arise if Wendy does not realise that the £1,680 maintenance is taxable. Small maintenance payments can pile up tax liability where the recipient does not know that she is supposed to include them in her tax return and pay tax on them – and then, three or four years later, she is faced with a massive back tax claim.

where there are children

Basically, children are treated in the same way for tax purposes as the spouse. The paying parent should

- always make maintenance payments under a court order – payments by a voluntary arrangement (or even under a legally binding agreement) are not tax effective
- always express the maintenance to be payable 'to the child' – not to the other parent 'for the child' or 'for the child's benefit'.

Provided these arrangements are followed, maintenance paid to the child will be treated as his or her income for tax purposes. Accordingly, the single person's tax allowance can be set against it so that £2,005 a year is free of tax. If the order were to the mother for the child, the payments for the child would count as hers for tax purposes. It is not necessary to open a special trust fund or bank account for the children. The mother can receive the money on their behalf as 'agent'. The important thing from the Inland Revenue's point of view is that the order is worded 'to the children' and not 'to the mother for the children'.

Where maintenance is payable under a court order, the order should be arranged to make use of the available personal tax allowances. For example, a separated wife with two small children have, between them, combined personal allowances of £7,165 namely:

	£
wife: single person's allowance	2,005
additional personal allowance for lone parent (APA)	1,150
1st child: single person's allowance	2,005
2nd child: single person's allowance	2,005
	£7,165

Therefore, if the husband were to submit to a court order for periodical payments of £3,155 p.a. to wife and £2,005 p.a. to each child of the family, the wife and the children would receive £7,165 p.a. tax free. At the same time, the husband would still be able to claim tax relief on all the maintenance he paid, as it is not regarded as his income for tax purposes.

Since child benefit is also not taxable (which for a single parent with two children for 1983/84 comes to £887 per annum), she can receive £8,052 by way of maintenance and child benefit without having to pay any tax on it. But she has to reclaim from the Inland Revenue the tax deducted by the husband from the maintenance payments to her and the children.

small maintenance payments for children

If an order for payment to a child is for a sum that does not exceed £33 a week or £143 a month, the payment counts as small maintenance and payments are made gross. For payment made to a spouse for the benefit of a child rather than to a child direct, the small maintenance limit is £18 a week or £78 a month.

If a court order specifies a certain amount for a spouse and certain amounts for each child, each amount is treated as a separate maintenance payment. So, for example, if a court orders £20 per week to be paid to a wife for herself and £20 to her for her child, the first will be treated as a small maintenance payment (because it is below £33 a week) and be paid gross, whereas the second will be treated as a 'large' maintenance payment (because it is above £18 a week for a child) and will be paid net of tax – the payer deducts 30% before making the payment.

example

Six years on, Harry and Wendy have two children, Charles aged three and Celia aged one; Harry is earning £12,000 p.a. and has agreed to an order to pay Wendy £3,500 p.a. for herself (payable monthly) and £1,000 p.a. (also payable monthly) each to Charles and Celia.

H's position

		£
total income		12,000
less: single person's tax allowance	2,005	
maintenance to Wendy	3,500	
maintenance to children	2,000	7,505
taxable income		4,495
H pays tax		
on own income at 30% on £4,495		1,349
on behalf of Wendy's maintenance at 30% on £3,500		1,050
		2,399

Over the year, Harry pays to Wendy £2,450 (£3,500 minus £1,050 tax deducted) for herself and £2,000 for the children.

Harry therefore has (£12,000 − £4,450 − £1,349) = £6,201

W's position

		£
total income: maintenance from H		3,500
less: single person's tax allowance	2,005	
additional personal allowance (APA)	1,150	
		3,155
taxable income		345

W is liable for tax at 30% on £345 = £104

But Harry has deducted £1,050 in tax, therefore Wendy has suffered too much tax and must reclaim £946 (£1,050 − £104) from the Inland Revenue.

Wendy therefore has:	£
from Harry	
for herself	2,450
for children	2,000
from Inland Revenue	946
plus child benefit	887
	6,283

Since both children are receiving less than £2,005 p.a. each, no tax is payable on the £2,000 maintenance to the children. If the order had been expressed to Wendy for the children, rather than to them, she would have had to pay 30% tax on the £2,000, reducing her income by £600 (to £5,683).

The figures can be juggled to make Wendy better off without affecting Harry's position:

● the family's overall tax liability can be reduced by diverting more of the maintenance to Charles and Celia: Harry can pay them each another £1,005 before any tax is payable

● the cash-flow for Wendy can be improved by as much as possible being paid gross under the small maintenance payments rule. Harry can increase the maintenance for Charles and Celia up to £1,716 each and reduce Wendy's maintenance to £2,068 per annum, on which no tax would be payable because it is less than her total tax allowances of £3,155. Wendy's maintenance would still not qualify as a small maintenance payment, therefore tax at 30% would be deducted at source by Harry. She would still have to make a tax repayment claim in respect of her own maintenance, but the overpaid tax would now be substantially reduced. Harry's tax position would be completely unaffected.

later effects

It might be argued that the order in the last example is slightly artificial in that it makes the maintenance for the children disproportionately high. There is a potential drawback in such an order for the husband or for the wife

— from a husband's point of view, if he were to agree to an order in this form, with disproportionately high payments to the children, and the wife were then to remarry, he might have difficulty in convincing the court that the orders for the children should now be reduced by a substantial downward variation because prior to the ex-wife's remarriage they were at an unrealistically high level in order to save tax

— from the wife's point of view, if she agrees to increase the children's maintenance and reduce her own for these reasons, when maintenance payments for older children cease, her own maintenance would be at a disproportionately low level.

It would therefore be prudent to ensure that the registrar keeps a note that the high maintenance for the children was agreed to relieve the wife of tax, in case she wishes to apply for an increase or the ex-husband wishes to apply for a downward variation.

Another slight problem might occur when the children became old enough themselves to understand the situation: an astute 14-year-old might insist that the £1,716 was his or hers to spend.

maintenance and higher rate taxpayers

Where the person who is paying maintenance earns a sufficiently high salary to come within the higher tax rates, the potential tax saving is even greater. When maintenance is made under a court order, it ceases to be counted the payer's income for tax purposes. For example, income that would be taxed in the payer's hands at 50% becomes the income of the wife or the children, and is likely to attract either no tax or only the standard rate of 30%.

example

Harry is a high flyer and, at the date of separation, he is earning £26,000 a year and Wendy is not working.

• *voluntary payments*

Harry voluntarily pays £7,500 p.a. to Wendy and £2,500 p.a. each to Charles and Celia.

H's position

Assuming that his only tax relief is the single person's allowance of £2,005, his taxable income is £23,995.

on taxable income of £15,400 tax is payable at 30%		£4,620
£ 2,800 tax is payable at 40%		£1,120
£ 4,900 tax is payable at 45%		£2,205
£ 895 tax is payable at 50%		£ 448
£23,995		£8,393

Harry therefore has (£26,000 − £8,393 − £12,500) = £5,107

W's position

total income:
  from Harry £12,500 plus child benefit £887 = £13,387 free of tax

• *under court order*

If the same sums are paid under a court order (the suggested maintenance order is purely illustrative and in no way represents the order that a court would necessarily make), the position is that Harry can now set not only his £2,005 single person's tax allowance but also the whole of the maintenance payment of £12,500 against his income. His taxable income is therefore £11,495.

	£
tax payable is: at 30% on £11,495	3,449
at 30% on Wendy's maintenance (£7,500)	2,250
at 30% on children's maintenance (£5,000)	1,500
	7,199

When Harry pays Wendy, he deducts tax at 30% on all the payments, and therefore pays her £5,250 plus £3,500 to the children.

Harry therefore has (£26,000 − £7,199 − £8,750) = £10,051

W's position

After deducting her personal tax allowances of £3,155 from the £7,500 maintenance, her taxable income is £4,345 on which she pays tax at 30% = £1,304.

Charles and Celia each have to pay tax on £495 (£2,500 − £2,005) at 30% = £297 in all.

The total tax bill for Wendy and the children is therefore £1,601 but since Harry has deducted £3,750 in all, Wendy is able to claim a tax repayment of £2,149.

		£
Wendy therefore has:		
from Harry		
for herself		5,250
for the children		3,500
from Inland Revenue		2,149
plus child benefit		887
		£11,786

Therefore, the overall tax bill is reduced by £3,343 because the maintenance is paid under a court order. Harry's net income has almost doubled, from £5,107 to £10,051 but Wendy's and the children's income has dropped by £1,601. The obvious thing to do is for Harry to offer commensurately more gross maintenance when switching from voluntary payments to a court order, so that the £3,343 gained is shared between both separated spouses. He will still be better off in net terms and she will gain, too, to compensate for the cash-flow problem.

In the above examples, the amount ordered by the court are illustrative and do not represent the order(s) a court would necessarily make.

---

making tax arrangements

Understanding how income tax works is important for two reasons. First, because you need to be able to calculate what your net position is going to be after tax and, second, because it enables you to take advantage of the system to save as much income tax as possible through the proper organisation of maintenance orders. You will need every penny you have when you are separated, so it is vital to make sure that you do not pay any more income tax than is absolutely necessary.

The golden rules are

● do not pay maintenance voluntarily for longer than necessary: make an enforceable agreement

● or get a court order at the earliest possible stage

● if paying maintenance towards the upkeep of children, spread the money between ex-spouse and children in such a way as to take maximum advantage of their respective personal tax allowances

● always make children's periodical payments payable to the child and not to the ex-spouse 'for the child's benefit'

● where appropriate, make use of the small maintenance payments provisions to avoid cash-flow problems for the recipient.

The procedure for financial arrangements

An application for financial provision can be made by the petitioner for the ancillary relief listed in the petition or by the respondent making an application after receiving a copy of the petition, or in the answer if defending. Leave of the court must be obtained before an application can be made by the petitioner for a request that was not in the petition.

after separation

Where a divorce is sought after a separation of five years or more, or on the basis of consent after a separation of at least two years, the respondent can indicate in the acknowledgment of service that he or she intends to apply to the court to consider what his or her financial position will be after the divorce. The decree cannot then be made absolute unless the registrar is satisfied that the petitioner is going to make fair and reasonable financial provision for the respondent, or the best that can be made in the circumstances.

A special form of application for the court to consider the respondent's financial position after the divorce can be obtained from the court office. It must be filed at the court to enable the respondent to gain the protection of these proceedings (an indication in the acknowledgment of service is not sufficient).

the orders

An application can be made for

★ an order for maintenance pending suit
★ a periodical payments order (for spouse and/or children)
★ a lump sum order (for spouse and/or children)
★ an order for secured provision (for spouse and/or children)
★ a property adjustment order.

An order for maintenance pending suit can be made by the court at any time after the petition is filed and comes into effect as soon as it is made or it can be back-dated to the date on which the petition was filed; similarly, an order for periodical payments for children. The other orders cannot be made until the decree nisi is pronounced and are not enforceable until the decree is made absolute.

The question of money is generally dealt with separately from that of the divorce. When financial matters drag on, especially if they end up in a hearing, it may be many months or even years before they are finally sorted out. As time is money and you are likely to be instructing solicitors, this is bound to be expensive.

A legal aid certificate covers work in connection with financial applications, including representation at the hearing.

If you have agreed financial arrangements between you, send a document embodying the agreed terms, signed by both of you (or your solcitors), when applying for directions for trial. If acceptable to the court, it will be possible for a consent order to be made at the same time as the decree nisi is pronounced.

Making an application

Although an application will not be considered by the court until the decree nisi, you should prepare for your application as early in the proceedings as possible.

If you are the petitioner, you apply by *Notice of intention to proceed with application for ancillary relief made in petition*; if you are the respondent, by *Notice of application for ancillary relief*. Both forms are available free from divorce court offices.

Two copies of the notice of application have to be completed (and keep an extra one for yourself) and both have to be lodged at the court office. There is a fee for lodging an application (at present, £12).

There is space on the form for filling in the date of the hearing: this will be done by the court office.

List the orders you are seeking. It is not necessary to state the amounts of the maintenance payments or lump sum claimed: these will be negotiated.

Where the application includes a property adjustment claim, the address of the house or flat or description of any other property which you wish to be transferred should be given and an affidavit in support of the application must be lodged with the application.

The application will be sealed at the court office and handed back to you. You must then send a copy of the application to your spouse (together with a copy of any affidavit you have lodged with the application), if possible within four days. Use recorded delivery or get a certificate of posting from the counter clerk at the post office. If your spouse does not turn up at the hearing, you will have to satisfy the court that the copy application was sent.

The notice of application requires the other spouse to file an affidavit of his or her means within 14 days of receiving the notice of application.

The applicant should also prepare an affidavit of means, using the standard form of affidavit (obtainable from the divorce court office, or – for a few pence – from law stationers shops: form Div 86). This should be completed in triplicate, the top copy lodged at the court, one copy sent to the other spouse, and one to keep. If there is already in existence a magistrates' court order for the maintenance of the other spouse or children, a copy should be sent with the affidavit to the divorce court. If the application is for maintenance and/or lump sum only, the affidavit should be filed within 14 days of the other spouse's affidavit, although it can be filed earlier.

the affidavits

The basis of the evidence before the registrar is contained in the affidavits sworn by each party. (The registrar is the person who deals with all financial and property applications to the divorce court.) It is therefore important to make sure that the information in your own affidavit is complete and accurate and gives all the information that the registrar is likely to require. It is equally important to ensure that your spouse discloses all relevant information.

affidavit of means

Clear and accurate details should be given of capital and of income and of expenditure, stressing the sort of outgoings or liability that the registrar may take into account in increasing or decreasing the one-third starting point.

It is usually helpful to attach to the affidavit copies of several recent payslips and of your P60 (the form issued to all employees in April of each year, giving details of gross pay and tax deducted). If you are self-employed, at least your three most recent sets of accounts should be provided.

Unless you are applying for a transfer of property order, it is not necessary to file an affidavit until your spouse has done so. If your affidavit is the second to be filed, you can comment on any omissions or inaccuracies in his or her affidavit.

If your spouse has failed to file an affidavit and you think he or she is going to continue to be difficult about this, do not allow matters to drift on too long; delaying may be a deliberate tactic. You can apply to the registrar for an order requiring that an affidavit be filed within a set period and to have what is known as a 'penal notice' endorsed on the order. If this is done and a copy of the order served personally on your spouse, he or she is in contempt of court if he or she fails to comply, and an application can be made to the judge to commit him or her to prison.

interim order

If your affidavit contains some reasonably up-to-date information about your spouse's financial position, this may enable the registrar to make at least an interim order even if your opponent has failed to file his or her affidavit in time.

If the wife has some evidence as to the husband's income and he does not file his affidavit or does not attend a hearing, the registrar could make an interim order based on her estimate of the husband's income and a general assessment of his likely liabilities. This may turn out to be a punitive order but it is not designed to be such.

On the other hand, if the husband is not cooperating at all, the registrar might well make a high interim order for periodical payments with the deliberate aim of forcing him to disclose his means in order to obtain a reduction of the order or to avoid enforcement proceedings. An interim order can be replaced by a lower (or higher) order which is then backdated to the date of the interim order.

for property adjustment

An applicant for a property adjustment order must file an affidavit at the time of the application. As much information as possible should be given in the affidavit about the property you wish to be transferred to you: its value, when it was bought and the price paid for it.

For a house, details should be given of any mortgages on it (including any insurance policy which is collateral security for a mortgage) and the amount still owing to the mortgagees, whether the title to the property is registered and, if so, the title number.

If it is necessary to have the property valued, it is usually best, if at all possible, to agree on a particular valuer to carry out the valuation and to accept that one valuation.

Where several houses have been owned during the marriage, try to give details of each and the dates of purchase and sale (approximately), the prices paid and obtained for each property and the contributions made by each spouse to the purchase (including loans or gifts by in-laws) or to the improvement of each home.

Also include any information you have about your spouse's other property.

information omitted

When you receive a copy of your spouse's affidavit, go through it carefully to see whether he or she has omitted any major assets or sources of income. If you think so, you can comment on this in a further affidavit.

If you want to see copies of the other's bank statements, building society account books, payslips, a self-employed person's accounts, or to find out when and for what price certain assets were acquired or sold, write and ask for this information. Rule 77(4) of the Matrimonial Causes Rules 1977 states: 'Any party to an application for ancillary relief may by letter require any other party to give further information concerning any matter contained in any affidavit filed by or on behalf of that other party or any other relevant matter, or to furnish a list of relevant documents or to allow inspection of any such document . . ..'

If the information is not supplied, you can then apply to the registrar asking him to order your opponent to provide such information or documents.

'directions' and preliminary hearing

Notification of the date of the hearing is sent by the court to both parties. It is important to be clear as to the nature of the hearing – preliminary or full. If unsure, make a telephone call to the clerk's office at the court to ask.

In many courts, particularly where the application includes a claim for a lump sum payment, there will first be a hearing at which the registrar gives directions for further requirements – for instance, what affidavits should be exchanged and when.

You yourself can apply for a hearing 'for directions' if one is not fixed – for instance, if your opponent has failed to comply with any request you had made under Rule 77, or had failed to file an affidavit or if there is delay and you want an interim order for maintenance. (But if the registrar feels that such a hearing was unnecessary, he may order you to pay your opponent's costs or expenses in attending the hearing.)

At a directions hearing, the registrar will not make a decision about the application (unless it is for an agreed or interim order) but will be concerned to ensure that the necessary steps have been or will be taken so that all the required information will be available to the court at the eventual hearing.

The registrar can make orders for further affidavits, for information or documents to be supplied, for discovery of documents relevant to the applications, for either or both parties to give oral evidence, for valuation, for giving notice to any mortgagee. Cohabitants cannot be ordered to file affidavits but they can be ordered to attend for examination at the final hearing and may be given leave to file affidavits instead if they wish.

If you want to be sure that your spouse will be present at the full hearing to give evidence, ask at the preliminary hearing for the registrar to make an order that he or she should attend for cross-examination.

The registrar can make an order for interim maintenance at this hearing if no maintenance, or insufficient voluntary maintenance, is being paid and he has some evidence of the means of both parties.

when there has been maintenance pending suit

An order for maintenance pending suit will cease when the decree is made absolute. Before this happens, the person receiving the maintenance should write to the court to ask for the order to be changed into a periodical payments order at the same rate (unless he or she wants to apply for an order for a different amount). The court gives notice of this to the payer. If he does not object, an order for periodical payments at the same rate is made without a hearing before the registrar.

If the payer does object, an appointment will be made for both sides to attend a hearing at which the registrar will decide the amount of the periodical payments to be ordered. Affidavits should be filed before the hearing, with up-to-date information about means.

the hearing

Before the final hearing, you should have prepared for your own use a summary of the financial position of each of you. From your joint gross income, work out the one-third starting figure, noting down any factors which you feel should in your case increase or decrease this starting point. Such a summary will help you to present your case clearly to the registrar; it will be useful to take along a copy to hand to him.

People who are dealing with their own case have to attend the hearing before the registrar. Make sure to bring all the relevant documents with you. Even people represented by lawyers are usually present to give evidence if required and to hear the registrar's decision.

The hearing is 'in chambers' – that is, not in open court. Each side has an opportunity to state his or her case.

You may have to give oral evidence, on oath, if only to bring the affidavit up-to-date. When there is oral evidence, the applicant gives evidence first and can be cross-examined by the other party – who can similarly be cross-examined on his or her evidence, if appropriate.

When oral evidence is not asked for, after the affidavits are read, both sides can make submissions or comments, but neither is subject to cross-examination.

the registrar's decision

Before deciding on the amount of maintenance to order, the registrar will take into account
★ the gross income of the husband
★ any necessary expenses of his work that can properly be set against his gross income
★ the gross income of the wife
★ any necessary expenses of her work that can properly be set against her gross income
★ broad details of the expense of maintaining the children
★ the needs and outgoings of husband and of wife
★ any particular expenditure of either or any particular circumstances that might lead to departure from the one-third starting point
★ the effect of tax on any proposed order
★ the effect of any order on supplementary benefit entitlement.
When dealing with a request for a property adjustment or a lump sum payment order (which may or may not be at the same hearing as for a maintenance order), the registrar will consider
★ the full extent of each party's capital and details of any other assets
★ the value of the matrimonial home, and any other properties owned by either the husband or the wife or by both
★ the amount owing on any mortgages
★ the needs of each for accommodation
★ the effect of any order on the statutory charge if husband or wife is legally aided
★ who has custody of the children
★ whether the matrimonial home is in the joint names of the couple or in one name only
★ the financial contributions or other contributions made by each towards the purchase or improvement of the matrimonial home and any previous homes.

The registrar makes his decision, possibly adjusting capital against income to produce the most sensible result in the circumstances of the particular family.

For periodical payments, he usually sets out the facts as he finds them about the income, assets and liabilities of each of the parties; he may use the one-third starting point for maintenance (or if he does not do so, indicate his reasons for departing from this).

If the registrar dismisses an application for periodical payments, it cannot later be revived. The applicant may have agreed to this in return for some other financial provision, such as a larger lump sum or transfer of the home. (At present, an order will not be dismissed without the applicant's consent; when the Matrimonial and Family Proceedings Bill comes into force, this may no longer be required.)

An order for costs to be paid by the other side can be asked for at this stage.

Make a written note of the registrar's judgment in case there should be an appeal. It may also be useful to have a note of the registrar's basis for arriving at the payments ordered – for instance, a low maintenance payment because the wife receives a larger share in the matrimonial home. This may be taken into account on any subsequent application to vary a maintenance order.

After the hearing, the court office prepares the order(s) and sends a copy to both parties. Check the wording and figures carefully, in case there is a clerical error. Then keep the documents in a safe place.

appeal
An appeal against an order or decision of the registrar can be made to a judge by filing a notice of appeal within five working days. The notice setting out the grounds should be prepared by a solicitor.

'registering' the order

It is possible to apply to the registrar for the order for maintenance to be registered in the magistrates' court of the area where you live or work. The purpose is to make enforcement simpler.

A statement, including the names and addresses of the parties and the amount of maintenance payable, must be lodged at the divorce court and a fee paid (at present, £2).

The maintenance order is sent to the magistrates' court and the payer then has to make all payments through that court, which keeps a record of them. If an order has fallen into arrear, the payee can request the clerk to the justices to take the necessary steps to enforce it.

When an order is registered, either party can apply to the magistrates' court instead of the divorce court to vary the order, or the payer can apply there to be let off any arrears.

If the request for registration in the magistrates' court is not made at the time of the maintenance order, an application can subsequently be made to the original divorce court. An affidavit must be filed giving full particulars of the names and addresses of the parties and any children, the amount of any arrears, and also the reason why registration in the magistrates' court is now required.

Where an order has been registered at the magistrates' court and the payer falls into arrear, the recipient can assign the order to the DHSS and get supplementary benefit instead.

The matrimonial home

The expression 'the matrimonial home' is used in the context of divorce to refer to the home – house or flat – acquired by husband or wife or both to be lived in by the family during their joint lives.

There are basically three kinds of order that the divorce court can make

● for a sale, with division of the proceeds

● for transfer of one spouse's interest to the other

● for a postponed sale – usually until the children complete their education but sometimes beyond that, the house then to be sold and the proceeds divided in specified proportions.

There are no laid-down principles as to when the court will make one or other of these orders or in what proportion it will order the proceeds of sale to be split. For every case where a sale and 50/50 division of the proceeds will be appropriate, there are many others where this would operate unfairly against one or other of the parties. The court's decision in each case largely depends on whether there are any children, the age of the parties, the length of the marriage and whether the spouse who will move out has potentially secure accommodation.

rented property

The divorce court has power to make a transfer of tenancy order on divorce with regard to any tenancy – private or local authority.

Many leases contain a clause that the tenancy should not be assigned without the landlord's consent. But the law provides that such consent should not be unreasonably withheld and if the court were to make a transfer order and the landlord objected, this would probably be evidence of withholding consent unreasonably. It would be wiser to obtain the landlord's consent, preferably in writing, before an application for transfer of the tenancy is made.

protected tenancy

Where a tenancy is a protected tenancy (within the Rent Act 1977) the court can order it to be transferred to the other spouse under the Matrimonial Causes Act 1973, just like any other property. Application can be made at decree nisi and an order will take effect on decree absolute.

statutory tenancy

Where a protected tenancy has become a 'statutory' tenancy (for example, because the landlord has served notice to quit on the occupying tenant – the husband or the wife or both of them), the tenant has a right to remain on the premises unless and until the landlord can obtain a possession order.

Although there would no longer be any 'property' in the understood sense, the wife (assuming the tenancy is in the husband's name) may still be able to obtain a transfer to her of the statutory tenancy under the Matrimonial Homes Act 1983 (in which case, notice has to be given to the landlord). It is vital, however, that the tenancy should be transferred before decree absolute because, once she is no longer the wife, if the husband has left home there will be no tenant in occupation within the meaning of the Act and thus the statutory tenancy will have lapsed.

council tenancy

Any such tenancy is 'property' and can be transferred under the Matrimonial Causes Act as part of the financial arrangements on divorce (also under the Matrimonial Homes Act). It is not possible simply to ask the local authority to adjust the tenancy (as used to be the case before the Housing Act 1980). Local authorities are more or less in the same position as private landlords when it comes to obtaining possession and if, for example, the house is in the husband's name, the local authority cannot merely serve notice to quit on the husband and give a new tenancy to the wife.

owner-occupied property

Although the court needs to assess what the financial interest of husband and wife is in the home, in most cases this is only the first stage of the process by which the court decides what is to happen.

Whose name the house is actually in – husband's, wife's or jointly – or who put up the deposit and who paid the mortgage is obviously important but is not necessarily the decisive factor. Taken into account are not only contributions to the buying but also to the maintenance of the home.

In the early stages of the marriage, particularly if there are no children, the court may look mainly at the financial contributions and decide that the person who put the most in should have the most out. But the longer the marriage has gone on, and especially if there are children, the less the court is interested in who put in what, in money terms, and the more it is prepared to recognise the other party's non-money contribution. For instance, the wife's contribution in bearing and bringing up children and in keeping the home going may count as much as the husband's financial contributions.

The court will look primarily at the needs and resources of the family with regard to accommodation.

where there are no children

If there are no children, the main consideration will be whether the net proceeds of sale of the house are likely to be sufficient to enable each spouse (with the aid of such mortgage loan as each might reasonably be expected to obtain) to buy an adequate new home. If so, the court may well order a sale without delay.

Even if one of them wants to stay on, the house may have to be sold where the combined resources of husband and wife are insufficient to keep up the mortgage repayments on the existing home and to provide accommodation for the other spouse.

Where the house had been bought from the local authority with a discounted mortgage and the house or flat is sold within 5 years of buying, you have to pay back to the local authority a percentage of the discount you were allowed.

share in the proceeds

If the only family asset is the matrimonial home, and it is in the sole name of one of the spouses, the other can probably claim at least a one-third interest in the house (unless the marriage has lasted only a short time). In an increasing number of cases, however, the courts find that the non-owning spouse has acquired a half interest in the home.

The court will take into account direct financial contributions by the non-owning spouse towards the purchase (payment of part of the deposit or part of the mortgage repayments) or improvement of the house, and also the indirect financial contribution – where, for example the wife has worked for part of the marriage and has used her earnings to pay some of the household bills, food, clothing or has paid her earnings into the couple's joint bank account.

If the wife's share would be insufficient to enable her to buy a new home, particularly if her earnings put her into a less favourable position for getting a mortgage, the court could order that the wife should get a greater share of the proceeds of sale. The court may compensate the husband by ordering lower maintenance payments to the wife – or none at all.

not selling

A sale of the matrimonial home may, however, not be the right solution. The expenses of selling and buying two other houses will have to be met, and the net proceeds of sale may not be sufficient to enable either spouse to buy another home. (Moreover, if either party was legally aided, the Law Society may claim part of the proceeds for the legal aid fund's statutory charge).

The court could order that the wife remain in the house

• until she wants to move out or cohabits (this normally means more than 6 months of living together) or marries again, or dies

or

• for a period of time specified by the court.

The house would then be sold, and the net proceeds divided in proportions decided by the court.

If she is not making the mortgage payments, the wife might be ordered to pay to the husband in the meantime something in the way of rent in respect of the husband's half (or other share) of the house. This 'occupation' rent would be taxable in the recipient's hands and may be little compensation to the husband for being kept from his capital, usually for many years.

An arrangement which leaves the wife with a degree of uncertainty as to her future home, and the husband having to wait a number of years to receive his capital while he has to continue paying maintenance, can cause bitterness. The courts try to avoid some of these difficulties by arranging a 'clean break': for example, the house is transferred outright to the wife and the husband compensated by the dismissal of the wife's claim for maintenance.

buying out the other spouse

An alternative 'clean break' arrangement is for the spouse who is going to remain in the house to buy out the departing spouse, by paying him or her a lump sum for the other's share in the house. If this is done by the remaining spouse borrowing the money or raising an extra mortgage, there will be tax relief on the interest.

If the person who has been bought out uses the money towards buying another house and borrows the rest on mortgage, he or she will get tax relief on the interest on a loan of up to £30,000. In other words, the former matrimonial home being no longer his or her residence, both spouses can take advantage of the full amount of tax relief on a house each.

The 'clean break' is, however, only really 'on' where
★ the current net value of the home is large enough to give the wife the option of staying on, or selling and taking on a lower mortgage on a cheaper property
★ the husband has sufficient resources (and/or is not too old to get a mortgage) to be able to start again with a new house
★ there are no children.

where there are children

The court's priority is that an adequate home should be provided for the children.

selling

It is unlikely that the court would order a sale unless selling the home would bring in enough money to buy another house for the parent who is going to have the children (usually the wife) to live there with them.

The house would have to be sold if the wife could not keep up the mortgage repayments with whatever assistance by way of maintenance the husband could finance. More economical accommodation would then have to be bought for her and the children out of the proceeds of selling the house.

not selling

To secure the house as a home for the children, the court may order the husband to transfer it into joint names if it has been in his sole name. When a house is in joint names, it cannot normally be sold without the agreement of the joint owners, but either party can apply to the High Court for an order to enforce a sale. To prevent this, the divorce court normally directs that the house shall not be sold for a specific period, while she and the children live there – usually until the youngest child reaches school-leaving age.

An alternative is to transfer the house into the wife's sole name subject to a charge securing to the husband whatever proportion of the net proceeds of (eventual) sale the court thinks proper. A 'charge' over the property means that when it is sold, the charge (which is like a mortgage) comes into effect and the other spouse will get his or her money out of the proceeds. The court generally orders that the charge is not enforceable for a specified period.

In either case, the court specifies at what point the husband can realise his interest in the house. This is likely to be when the youngest child of the family comes of age or sometimes when the child who is normally resident in the home finishes undergoing full-time education. The husband may be given the right to apply to enforce the sale or the charge at any time if the ex-wife marries again or cohabits. If she has to borrow the money to pay off the charge (without selling the house), she will not get tax relief on the interest on the loan.

selling later

A difficult problem is whether the house should be kept as a home for the ex-wife even after the children have left home. The court will take into account whether the wife's share of the proceeds if the house were sold then would enable her to buy another house, and also the husband's need for the capital. The court can make only a guesstimate of what the situation is likely to be possibly 12 or 15 years ahead – what money the ex-wife would receive from the sale of the house, her likelihood of employment and earnings and mortgage capacity. Her share would need to be sufficient for her to buy a flat or a smaller house at an age when she is unlikely to be able to raise much by way of mortgage on, probably, low earnings. Meanwhile, the husband will have been able to start afresh with another mortgage because of his lower age and higher earnings at the time of divorce.

(When the house is eventually sold, liability for capital gains tax may arise for the ex-spouse who is still a joint-owner but who had moved out of the house.)

If it seems likely that the ex-wife will have insufficient to enable her to buy another house then, the court may well defer the sale (or enforcement of the ex-husband's charge) for the remainder of her life (or until she marries or cohabits) unless by not selling, the ex-husband's problems are likely to outweigh the ex-wife's.

Where either party was legally aided, the legal aid fund's statutory charge will not be levied until the house is sold. By then, inflation may have reduced the practical effect of the charge.

If she is paying off the mortgage on the house, the wife will be contributing to the value of the husband's eventual share of the proceeds of sale. If, however, there is no mortgage to be paid off, she will effectively be living in the house at the ex-husband's expense. The court therefore may make an order requiring her to pay the ex-husband an occupation rent from the time that the children cease to need the house as a home.

if mortgaged

Mortgages cannot simply be transferred and the court has no power to order the transfer of a mortgage – only the property subject to the mortgage. The consent of the building society or other mortgagee is necessary, otherwise the mortgagor (usually the husband) remains liable for the mortgage even if the property is transferred. The mortgagees must be served with notice of an intended application to the court for a transfer of ownership and have the right to object.

The building society or other mortgagee must agree before the transfer can take effect, and may require that any arrears be paid off. If the mortgagees do not agree to the transfer, it will be necessary to pay off the mortgage and find a new mortgagee.

It may well be the wife who is going to be responsible for meeting the mortgage repayments in future, possibly out of an income from maintenance payments on which the building society would not have agreed to make a mortgage loan. It is advisable for a wife to contact the building society as soon as possible and discuss ways of making repayments if and when the house is transferred. It is not uncommon for building societies to exercise their right to change the mortgage from an endowment basis to a repayment basis.

A mortgage on an endowment basis is linked to an insurance policy that will pay out enough to repay the loan (with a surplus if it is a with-profits policy) at the end of the mortgage term or on the policyholder's death. The application for a property adjustment order where there is an endowment mortgage should include an application to transfer the husband's beneficial interest in the insurance policy to the wife. If this is not transferred and she were to sell the house before the end of the mortgage term, the wife could get nothing from the policy and would have to pay off the whole mortgage loan out of the proceeds of sale. When the mortgage term comes to an end, a decision has to be made regarding any bonuses on the policy over the amount required to repay the loan. This surplus could be ordered to go to the husband to compensate for the loss of use of capital, or to the wife who has been paying the premiums for many years, or to be shared between them.

tax relief on mortgage interest

On a loan to buy (or improve) your home, tax relief is available on the whole of the interest on up to £30,000 of loan. If the loan exceeds £30,000, interest on the excess is not eligible for tax relief. So, a loan of £40,000, attracts tax relief on only three-quarters of the interest.

Where the loan does not exceed £30,000, the 30% tax relief is deducted from the monthly interest payable to the building society or other lender. This is known as 'mortgage interest relief at source' (MIRAS).

Tax relief is available only if the property is the only or main residence of yourself or of your former (or separated) spouse and you still retain an interest in the former home yourself.

If you transfer the former home to your spouse outright and go on making the mortgage payments direct, you would not qualify for the tax relief. (Only if the house were still in joint names would you get tax relief if you paid the mortgage interest direct.) Therefore if you wish to contribute to the mortgage payments on the matrimonial home, it would make sense to pay the extra to your former spouse in the form of maintenance because on this you will get tax relief.

If on divorce or separation your ex-spouse takes over the former matrimonial home and the responsibility for repayment of the mortgage, you will be free to get the full amount of tax relief on any mortgage up to £30,000 taken out by yourself to buy a new home.

Procedure for property adjustment

If husband and wife can come to an agreement about the division of their property, the court can be asked to approve the agreement. In cases of dispute, an application can be made to the court to decide the fairest arrangement; where the home is a tenancy, the landlord may have to be notified of the application.

An application for an adjustment or transfer of property order must be accompanied by an affidavit giving details of the property, including details of any mortgages on it and whether or not the title to the property is registered. (Once such an application has been made, it should be registered as a pending action against the property at the Land Registry or Land Charges Department, as appropriate.)

If the value of the home is not known or cannot be agreed, the court will usually direct that the property be valued. It saves money to agree who is to do the valuation rather than having one each.

If an order is made for the transfer of the whole of the home into the other spouse's name or from one into the joint names; a transfer or conveyance will have to be drawn up. Where a solicitor is required for the conveyancing, the work can be done under the green form scheme or a legal aid certificate.

when the house is to be sold

Where the court orders a sale and a division of the proceeds, the respective shares can be expressed in percentage terms, or fixed figures.

A percentage share may be the better decision. If one party agreed to accept a fixed sum from the proceeds of sale and the property fetches far more than was anticipated, he or she would lose out and it would be impossible to rectify this because the court has no power to vary a property order once it is made.

A fixed figure may be ordered, however, where the court awards the wife a higher share solely in order that she can buy a house. It is then usually better if the order is for payment of a specific sum, carefully calculated to take account of possible delays in sale. If that were not done and the property sold for less than anticipated, the whole point of the exercise would be defeated.

If the court believes that one spouse will not, or cannot, pay maintenance, it may make over all the proceeds of sale to the non-owning spouse in lieu of maintenance.

Sometimes it is possible to 'horse trade' capital for maintenance. For example, a wife who owns a half share in the matrimonial home may be prepared to forgo maintenance in return for receiving the husband's half share. If so, she must agree that her application for periodical payments for herself be dismissed.

The contents of the home

An application for a property adjustment order can, and should, include the contents of the family home. The person who is to remain in the home should apply to have the essential furniture and furnishing of the house transferred to her or him. Any agreement as to contents could be included in the order about the house, to avoid later uncertainty.

A sensible, practical approach is to negotiate who is to have what and then ignore these assets when calculating maintenance from money resources. However, if the wife accepts that the husband should have, for example, the set of Chippendale chairs, because they belonged to his family, then their value would be relevant in the eventual adjustment of capital.

Remember that items on hire purchase still unpaid for cannot be transferred to another name.

Where both husband and wife have similar assets, these do not necessarily cancel each other out. For example, where the husband has a company car and the wife has the family car, some adjustments may have to be made to allow for the fact that
★ husband does not have to pay for maintenance of the company car
★ a lot of this private mileage may be paid for
★ he may have free membership of a motoring organisation
★ his insurance and road tax may be paid for
but he does not have an asset he can sell, whereas the wife's car can be sold.

An inventory with estimated values is useful, preferably prepared jointly or by one side for agreement by the other. Whether it is worth getting an expert valuation depends on the amount or value involved, the cost of the valuation, and the degree of dispute. It is rarely worth getting an expert valuation unless the items are of great value, such as antiques or valuable pictures.

disputes

If you cannot agree on anything else, try to agree about the splitting up of the contents – furniture and effects. It will never be worth fighting this out in court unless there are some exceptionally valuable items.

Do not go to court to resolve disputes over furniture, the car, or other belongings, if you can possibly avoid it. It is nearly always preferable to come to your own agreement. Court proceedings over furniture or household belongings are nearly always protracted and expensive out of all proportion to the value of the property. They can result in a decision that is not what either party really wanted, and can lead to a forced sale.

ownership

Under section 17 of the Married Women's Property Act 1882, an application can be made to the county court or the High Court by either of the spouses at any time up to 3 years after the decree absolute, even if the applicant has married again, to resolve the question of the ownership of any property (other than the house, if this has been dealt with in the divorce).

When determining whether an applicant has an interest at all in the disputed property and, if so, how much, the court will take into account any contribution made by either spouse to its purchase or improvement, in the form of cash or physical work. Proof of where the money came from that was used to buy an item is important.

When it is necessary to determine the ownership of pieces of furniture, jewellery, antiques or similar belongings under the Married Women's Property Act, the court is likely to decide that

● any items owned by either of the couple before the marriage remain the property of that person

● any items subsequently bought by either spouse out of his or her own money are the property of that person

● any items bought jointly are jointly owned

● any items bought by the wife out of savings from her housekeeping money are jointly owned

● any assets bought out of a joint bank account into which both have paid money are jointly owned

● gifts to one of the couple remain his or her property

● gifts to both belong normally to the person from whose side of the family the gift came; where the gift was from a common friend, it is usually held to be jointly owned (this applies not only to wedding presents).

Under the Married Women's Property Act, the court can only establish who is the owner of the property. It can then order that the property be handed over to the established owner or that, if jointly owned, it be sold. It can direct how the proceeds shall be divided, but only according to strict legal principles: it does not have discretion to take all the circumstances into account as a court has under divorce legislation, nor to make a transfer of property order.

Capital gains tax

Capital gains tax (CGT) is payable at the rate of 30% on gains arising from the 'disposal of assets'.

The first £X,XXX of gains in any one tax year are exempt (in the 1984/85 tax year, £5,600). Only one lot of £5,600 is allowed per husband and wife (not £5,600 each) while they are married and for the remainder of the tax year in which they separate. Inflation is taken into account in assessing gains by reference to increases in the retail prices index (RPI) based on the figure at March 1982.

'Assets' means practically everything capable of being owned and sold or transferred. On divorce or separation, the major areas where disposals of property are likely to arise are
★ household contents
★ other assets such as car, a second home, stocks and shares, savings
★ the home.

household contents

Most consumer goods decrease in value, so the question of 'gain' does not arise. Most chattels with a lifespan of less than fifty years are exempt from CGT, anyway.

other assets

Cash and cars are specifically exempt from CGT, and so are any sums received on the surrender of life insurance policies. So if, for one reason or another, you cash in an endowment policy which is linked to a mortgage, there is no question of liability to CGT.

If there are other assets, such as stocks and shares, or interests in a business, a sale to raise cash gives rise to CGT. But if they are transferred between spouses, they would give rise to CGT liability only on subsequent disposal (unless the assets are transferred after the end of the tax year in which the couple separated).

the home

Any gain made on the sale of a person's principal private residence (PPR) is normally exempt from CGT.

You are likely to do one or other of three things

• sell it and split the proceeds

• transfer it to your spouse outright

• put it into joint names (or leave it in joint names) and postpone sale and division of the proceeds until a future date.

sale and division of proceeds

If you sell the house and split the proceeds within two years of one or other of you ceasing to reside there, you will be entitled to claim 'principal private residence' exemption provided the home was your only, or main, residence throughout the period that you owned it. Normally, CGT liability arises when a house is sold if you stopped living there more than two years ago.

If at any time you have two or more homes, both are potentially eligible for the exemption. If, therefore, you have bought another home and the old home has not been sold, you may have to make a choice as to which one you wish to have treated as your principal private residence. This choice has to be made within two years of acquiring the second residence. Normally, it would make sense to claim the exemption in respect of the house that is being sold, if this is at a gain.

Where the sale takes place more than two years after one of you has left, the person who ceased to reside there will not be fully exempt: only a portion of the gain will be exempt, namely the period of his or her actual occupation plus the last two years of ownership. (The last two years of ownership are always exempt.) Thus, the longer you wait beyond two years after separation before selling your old home, the greater the possibility of CGT being payable by the person who left. The person who remains will not be liable to CGT provided he or she has remained permanently in residence.

You will be liable to CGT on gain if you left the home more than two years ago, and either your old home was bought before April 1982 or it was bought after 1982 and, on selling it, you make a profit considerably grerater than the increase in the retail prices index since then.

Liability to CGT can be quite considerable if you and your spouse split up a long time ago and have only now got round to doing something about selling the house.

example

Herbert and Wilma had bought their first home for £7,000 in 1970. They separated in 1973 but only came to sell the house in March 1983 when it was sold for £36,500.

The house is in joint names and it is Wilma who has remained there. She has no CGT liability because she can claim PPR exemption on her share for the whole period.

Calculation of Herbert's CGT liability would be in two stages.

i) his net gain

This will be half of the difference between the cost of acquisition and the proceeds of sale, with an allowance for inflation between March 1982 and March 1983. The RPI on those dates was 313.4 and 327.9 respectively, an increase of 14.5 points.

(The value of the retail prices index is published monthly by the Department of Employment and the figures to be used in calculating the indexation allowance for the month of the sale of a house are obtainable from the Inland Revenue press office, Somerset House, London WC2R 1LB.)

The allowance is arrived at by adding to the cost of acquisition (the price he paid when he bought it) a sum calculated as follows:

$$\text{cost of acquisition} \times \frac{\text{increase in RPI March 82 to March 83}}{\text{RPI March 82}}$$

$$\text{i.e. } £7,000 \times \frac{14.5}{313.4} = £324$$

Herbert's net gain for capital gains tax purposes is therefore $\frac{£36,500 - £7,324}{2} = £14,588$

ii) his exemption

The formula to work out the amount that is exempt under the principal private residence exemption is

$$\text{gain} \times \frac{\text{years of occupation} + \text{last 2 years of ownership}}{\text{period of ownership}}$$

$$\text{i.e. } £14,588 \times \frac{3 + 2}{13} = £5,611$$

This reduces Herbert's gain to £8,977 of which £5,000 (the exemption for the tax year 1982/83) is exempt under the annual exemption rule. This leaves a taxable gain of £3,977.

Herbert's CGT liability on £3,977 at 30% is £1,193.

Capital gains tax would have been more of an expense if the house had been in Herbert's sole name. The whole of the net gain (£29,176) would then have been his, and the taxable gain would have been £11,222 − £5,000 exemption, giving a tax liability of £1,867. (In such a case, an accountant or solicitor might have advised him to argue that Wilma had acquired an interest in the home during the intervening period because she had, for example, been paying the mortgage.)

transfer of the home to your spouse outright

Although no money changes hands, the transfer would in theory be a 'disposal', based on the market value at the date of disposal. Quite apart from the fact that there may well not be a capital gain anyway (after taking inflation into account and the current £5,600 exemption), the transaction would qualify for PPR exemption if made within two years of the transferor leaving the house.

Even if the transfer were made outside the two year period, provided it was made as part of a divorce settlement and provided that you had not elected to declare any other home as your principal private residence, the Inland Revenue would treat the disposal as exempt by 'concession'. Therefore, provided you get the sequence right, i.e. *first* transfer your interest and *second* buy your new home (if you can afford it), liability to CGT will not arise.

house in joint names sold much later

Putting the house into joint names will not attract CGT liability, on the same principle as when there is a transfer.

When the house is sold many years later and the proceeds divided, the spouse who has remained in the home will not have to pay tax on his or her share because that will be fully covered by the PPR exemption. But the one who moved out will be liable to some CGT. In such a case, to save CGT, it would be worth transferring the house fully to the ex-spouse who is living there (subject to a charge to the other ex-spouse). It very much depends on which would give him the biggest potential tax saving.

second home

A second home can be more of a problem. Selling it to raise money may render you liable to capital gains tax if there is a sufficient gain. So, transferring it to the spouse who is moving out of the matrimonial home would make more sense, especially if he or she proposed to live in it as his or her principal private residence, so that if and when it is eventually sold, it will be possible to claim PPR exemption on the whole of any gain – provided the transfer takes place before the end of the tax year in which the spouses separate. (After that, the transferor will have a CGT liability by reference to the market value of the property at the time of the transfer.)

advice

You may well feel that you need specialist advice about capital gains tax, perhaps from an accountant. For someone in receipt of legal aid, it might be better for the solicitor to instruct the accountant since he will then pay the accountant's fee and can recover the fee from the legal aid fund as an expense reasonably incurred. If the accountant were instructed directly, the client would have to find the money more or less straightaway (whereas a legal aid charge may not be payable until considerably later, if at all).

Scotland and Northern Ireland

This book deals only with the situation in England and Wales. Here are some very brief indications about Northern Ireland and Scotland.

Northern Ireland

The principal order in Northern Ireland is the Matrimonial Causes (Northern Ireland) Order 1978. The law and procedure in matrimonial proceedings in Northern Ireland is, generally speaking, the same as in England and Wales. However, there are some differences, the main ones being that

• there are no 'postal' or 'special procedure' divorces in Northern Ireland: the parties must attend the court in person and give their evidence to the judge

• undefended divorces are available in Northern Ireland in both the High Court and county court at the choice of the petitioner

• legal aid is available in Northern Ireland for all the divorce proceedings

• the Matrimonial Homes Act does not apply to Northern Ireland.

Scotland

The ground for divorce is basically the same in Scotland as England, but the procedure and terminology are quite different. The person seeking the divorce is called 'the pursuer' and the other spouse 'the defender'.

There is no minimum period of marriage before a divorce can be applied for; no formal reconciliation procedure, or delay for attempted reconciliation. Decree of divorce when granted is equivalent to the 'decree absolute' – there is no such thing in Scotland as 'decree nisi', although a decree can be appealed against within 21 days of having been granted.

Divorces may be raised in any sheriff court or in the Court of Session in Edinburgh.

quickie divorces

Where a couple wishes to proceed with a two year consent divorce or a five year divorce, and there are no children of the marriage, or none under 16 years of age, and neither party is making any financial claims, they can proceed by the 'quickie procedure'. The necessary printed forms can be obtained from the court.

In two year consent divorces, the pursuer fills in part 1 of the form and sends it to the other spouse who completes part 2 indicating his or her consent. On receipt of that, the pursuer completes the affidavit in part 3, swearing the affidavit before a notary public (most solicitors are notaries public) or a justice of the peace, then forwards to the court the completed forms with the extract marriage certificate (photocopies are not acceptable) and a remittance for the court dues. The court takes all the administrative steps (of service etc.) from then on and advises the parties when decree of divorce is granted. No appearance of the parties in court is necessary.

In five year separation divorces, the procedure is similar but consent is not necessary and part 2 is in the form of an affidavit which is sworn before a notary public or justice of the peace.

The court dues are at present £42. Any pursuer who is either in receipt of supplementary benefit or of legal advice and assistance ('pink form' legal aid) does not need to pay the court dues.

non-quickie divorces

Where there are children of the marriage under 16 years of age and/or the pursuer is making financial claims, it is necessary to go through a more complicated procedure and you should get the advice of a solicitor.

Legal aid is available, both under the legal advice and assistance scheme – the pink form scheme (the equivalent of the 'green form' scheme in England) – in connection with obtaining the necessary evidence, and – under a certificate known as a 'section one' certificate – for the court proceedings themselves. Legal aid limits are relatively generous and you should always insist that the solicitor checks your eligibility for legal aid. Unlike England, any 'section one' legal aid certificate issued is backdated to the date when the application for legal aid was received by the appropriate legal aid committee.

A summons or initial writ is lodged in court and served on the other party by the pursuer's solicitor. If the case is to be defended, the opponent (defender) has to intimate to the court that he or she is defending the case, and thereafter lodge defences, and the case proceeds to hearing.

If the action is not defended, the divorce proceeds by way of 'affidavit procedure'. The pursuer and a supporting or corroborating witness have to swear affidavits which are lodged in court. If the judge is satisfied with the evidence, decree of divorce will be granted.

The pursuer's affidavit also has to deal with arrangements for any children of the marriage under 16 years of age and to narrate as far as is known the financial position of both parties. Where there are children involved, an affidavit has to be lodged and sworn by a person who is not a party to the action, speaking to the accommodation available for the children, and speaking generally to the welfare of the children. This affidavit can be sworn by a person who is a near relative, perhaps the grandmother or grandfather of the children.

In an undefended action, even where there are children involved, it is not necessary for the pursuer to appear in court or before a judge in chambers. If the judge is satisfied with the affidavits, including the evidence about the arrangements for the welfare of the children, decree of divorce will be pronounced.

financial claims

Maintenance for a wife or husband is called 'periodical allowance', maintenance for children is called 'aliment'. A lump sum payment is called a 'capital payment'.

lump sum

In Scotland, once decree of divorce has been granted, it is not possible to apply to the court for a capital payment or a property transfer order. It is very important, therefore, to seek legal advice before raising proceedings to see whether you would be able to seek a lump sum payment. This depends on a variety of factors such as the length of the marriage, the respective conduct of the parties, and the respective positions of the parties so far as savings are concerned, including the ownership of heritable property.

maintenance

The pursuer can apply to the court in the divorce proceedings for maintenance (that is, periodical allowance). The defender also can apply for maintenance, although it is less likely that he or she will be granted an award of maintenance by the court.

The extent of any award of periodical allowance by the court depends on the conduct of the parties, the length of the marriage and the financial position of the parties.

variation

After decree of divorce has been pronounced, application can be made to vary the maintenance award or to obtain a maintenance award where there was no award in the original proceedings, but this depends on the applicant satisfying the court that there has been a material change in circumstances. The variation may be upwards or downwards. Any right of an ex-spouse to maintenance ceases on his or her death or remarriage.

for children

Claims for maintenance for children should be made in the divorce proceedings by the person having custody of the children. For example a defender spouse may have custody which is not in dispute. In that event, he or she can defend the proceedings to get a formal award of custody from the court and to obtain aliment (that is, maintenance for the children). In addition, application can be made both for non-residential and residential (staying) access by any party showing an interest.

tax consequences

Tax relief is granted on maintenance payments under a court order. It is important to seek advice to make sure maintenance orders are arranged in such a way as to obtain the most advantageous tax benefits.

So far as maintenance for children is concerned, you should ask your lawyer to consider making claims for maintenance for children under the 'Huggins' formula as this can substantially reduce the tax payable. By this means, maintenance payments for children are made to the custodial parent in trust for the children; the parent is not assessed for tax on the payments which count as the child's income and eligible for each child's personal tax allowance.

the home before divorce

It is important to seek legal advice as to the extent of any rights of occupancy you might have under the Matrimonial Homes (Family Protection) (Scotland) Act 1981, because once you are no longer married, these rights cease. For example

● the wife who is not tenant of the matrimonial home (and her husband is) has occupancy rights and cannot be excluded from the home

● the wife who is not the joint owner of the matrimonial home has occupancy rights and cannot be excluded.

There are important provisions about court orders for transfer of tenancy, exclusion of violent spouses, and other aspects regulating rights in the matrimonial home. For example, a joint owner can be prevented from forcing a sale of the matrimonial home.

Costs

Costs may be 'party-and-party' or 'common fund' or 'solicitor-and-own-client'.

party-and-party costs are the costs the solicitor can recover for his client when there is a court order for costs against the other side: usually about 75% of all reasonable costs.

common fund costs is what the solicitor can charge the legal aid fund under a legal aid certificate; he can charge for a greater amount of work than for party-and-party costs but at the same charging rate as for party-and-party costs.

solicitor-and-own-client costs is what a solicitor will charge you as his privately paying client: the full amount of all reasonable costs at his own charge-out rate.

Privately paying clients are always liable for their own solicitor's fees, 'win' or 'lose'. Even if they get an order for their costs to be paid by the other side, this will not cover everything.

You are entitled to query your solicitor's bill and to ask for a fully itemised account, with details of time spent and disbursements. If still dissatisfied, you are entitled to have the costs 'taxed' on a solicitor-and-own-client basis.

taxation of costs

Taxation is the process whereby the registrar at the county court considers the bill and decides whether the charges made are fair and reasonable in the circumstances of the particular case. The solicitor-and-own-client basis disallows costs 'insofar as they are of an unreasonable amount or have been unreasonably incurred'. The solicitor's bill may have to be reduced accordingly.

A solicitor is not entitled to sue for his or her bill on a contentious matter unless he gives a month's notice to the client with a reminder of the client's right to have the bill taxed.

Extract from a solicitor's bill for taxation

BETWEEN   VAT registration number

.....................................Petitioner

and

.....................................Respondent

Petitioner's bill of costs for taxation on a Common Fund basis pursuant
to Second Schedule to Legal Aid Act 1974. Order dated...................

Civil Aid Certificate dated.................. No...................
                                          amended ....

Item
Number   Date   Chronological Table

PART I   PROCEEDING IN HIGH COURT
                        Preparation for Trial on behalf of Petitioner –
                        dealing with ways of obtaining divorce without
                        proceeding on a fully defended basis and also with
                        financial matters
                        Work charged @ £xx per hour; letters out and
                        telephone calls @ £x.xx each; letters in @ £.xx

                        The Client
                        Attending her prior to and after the Conference
                        with Counsel (30 minutes)
                        Personal attendance   1 (30 minutes)
                        Telephone attendances   6
                        Letters out – 6
                                 in – 3
                                                    (£xx.xx)

                        Other Parties
                        Correspondence generally regarding
                        maintenance, matrimonial home etc, involving
                        lengthy correspondence in an effort to reach an

agreement regarding the division of the
matrimonial home
Telephone attendances 8
Letters out – 12
  in – 6
(£xx.xx)

Considering papers prior to Conference with
Counsel and also consideration of financial
matters prior to writing lengthy letter to
Respondent's Solicitors (3 hours in all)
(£xx.xx)

TOTAL PART A – £xxx.xx
General care and attention @ 50%
TOTAL PART B – £xx.xx
Taxation of costs (part)

PART II

PROCEEDING IN COUNTY COURT
Preparing instructions to Counsel to settle
Affidavit for property transfer order etc

Photocopy documents to accompany (30)
 Paid Counsel – affidavit
     – application
     – advice

Top copy affidavit in support (13 sheets)

Two photocopies (26 sheets)
 Paid oath

Top copy application

Two photocopies
 Paid fee

Instructions to Counsel to advise

Attending Conference with Counsel

Attending Hearing with Counsel when orders
made
 Paid Counsel – Brief
     – Conference

PREPARATION FOR TRIAL on behalf of Petitioner – dealing with complex financial situation, heavily defended by Respondent, resulting in an order to transfer to Petitioner on payment of £xxxx. Thereafter dealing with difficulties over the transfer.

A considerable amount of work was necessary in this matter.

Work charged @ £xx.xx per hour; letters out and telephone calls @ £x.xx each; letters in @ £.xx each

The Client

Attending her discussing matters generally (20 minutes)

Attending her discussing Counsel's draft affidavit and generally (2 hours)

Attending her on her swearing Affidavit (20 minutes

Attending her going through Respondent's affidavit at length (45 minutes)

Attending her discussing documents required by Respondent's solicitors (20 minutes)

Attending her discussing (35 minutes)

Attending her discussing terms of order (15 minutes)

Personal attendances 7 (4 hours 35 minutes)

Telephone attendances 19

Letters out – 35

      in – 10   (£xxx.xx)

Other Parties

Correspondence with Respondent's Solicitors, with HM Inspector of Taxes, and generally

Attending Counsel and discussing (engaged 20 minutes)

Attending Respondent's Solicitors (engaged 20 minutes)

Correspondence in an effort to settle matters

Arranging to obtain a valuation of the property

Correspondence re contents of matrimonial home

Dealing with the transfer of the property to the Petitioner

Personal attendances 2 (40 minutes)

Telephone attendances 27

Letters out – 55

    in – 28   (£xxx.xx)

Considering figures etc provided by Petitioner prior to Brief etc (1 hour)

Preparing documents and considering (1 hour)

                  (£xx.xx)

TOTAL Part A – £xxx.xx

General care and attention @ 50%

TOTAL Part B – £xxx.xx

DEALING WITH TRANSFER OF MATRIMONIAL HOME TO PETITIONER including attendances upon Petitioner and Respondent's solicitors, postages, telephone calls and incidentals

Disbursements:

Land Charges – search fee

Stamp Duty on conveyance

Taxation of costs (part)

SUMMARY

PART I

Less taxed off

Add VAT on Profit Costs @ 15%

PART II

Less taxed off

Add VAT on Profit Costs @ 15%

Add Disbursements

Total Part II

Add Part I

Add taxing fee

TOTAL BILL =

For taxation, the bill has to be drawn up in a specially detailed form, in chronological order of the steps taken.

Certain items – for example, preparation and copying of documents – are charged at fixed rates; the bulk of the bill will be based on the hours spent by the solicitor preparing the case for hearing, with a mark-up for what solicitors call 'care and attention'. The basic hourly rate depends on the firm of solicitors and the area of the country (anything from £25 to £100); the mark-up, on the importance of the subject matter (anything from 33% to 60%).

The solicitor can charge for drawing up a bill for taxation, and also for attendance at court to determine the figure to be paid. There is a court fee for the taxation of costs: so-many pence (currently 5p) per £ of the final taxed costs.

costs awarded

When an order for costs is made, it is usual for the bill to be taxed, on a party-and-party basis. This should be done within 3 months of the date of any order for costs.

If you want your spouse to pay at least a part of your legal costs, a request 'for costs' should be made at each stage of the proceedings, whenever orders are sought.

In divorce matters, there is not just one set of proceedings: apart from the obtaining of the decree, there are matters of litigation on maintenance, property adjustment, custody, access – all of which run up costs, and all of which may be subject to different kinds of orders. At the conclusion of each such hearing, you can ask the registrar or judge for an order for costs and he decides there and then whether to make such an order.

If someone on legal aid is ordered to pay the other party's costs, the legal aid certificate does not cover this: the person has to pay out of his or her own pocket. The court must determine the amount that is reasonable for the legally aided person to pay. It may limit the amount of such costs to the equivalent of the person's legal aid contributions and make the costs payable over 12 months. Sometimes, the amount of the wife's share in the property is increased to take account of her liability for her own costs rather than an order for costs made against the husband.

• *for the divorce*

The petitioner can ask for costs if the divorce is based on adultery, unreasonable behaviour or desertion.

Where the divorce is obtained under 'the special procedure', the respondent (or in the case of adultery, the co-respondent) will not normally be required to pay more than the amount fixed by the Matrimonial Causes (Costs) Rules – generally no more than £125. In any normal run-of-the-mill case not involving unavoidable unusual expenditure, the petitioner's solicitor has his charges assessed by reference to this scale.

example

W goes to see a solicitor to obtain a simple divorce based on H's adultery. She has to settle up with her own solicitor. She obtains an order for costs, assessed at £125. Supposing she had insisted on 'five star' service, requiring the solicitor to come personally to her house, spending many hours discussing the matter, and speaking to him or her many times on the telephone to find out how the case was progressing, it is possible that her solicitor's bill comes to £400. W will have to pay the £275 difference herself. A similar situation could arise where W, instead of consulting local solicitors, had instructed expensive London solicitors to conduct the divorce for her: again, this is a luxury for which she herself must pay.

• *for an injunction*

The proceedings can run up very substantial costs. Normally, the successful applicant should obtain an order for costs against the respondent. But in many cases, this may not be worth the paper it is written on, either because the respondent disappears or because the applicant has no wish to cause further trouble by enforcing the order for costs.

● *custody and access*

Considerable costs can be run up in disputes over custody and access. The fact that one parent obtains custody rather than the other does not necessarily mean that that parent has 'won' in the same sense as would be the case in, for example, a claim for damages for personal injuries. So, both parties may be left to bear their own costs. The court is only likely to order one party to pay the other's costs if that one's behaviour during the proceedings has been in some way unreasonable.

● *financial matters*

There is no set principles as to the making of an order for costs. The mere fact that the wife obtains an order for maintenance or an order relating to the matrimonial home does not necessarily mean that she will be awarded costs. If an order is made, on a party-and-party taxation, a successful litigant will normally get paid by the other side about 80% of the original total bill.

Sometimes, a husband's solicitors will at an early stage offer to pay the wife's costs (sometimes even on a solicitor-and-own-client basis) in order to force a settlement.

example of how costs may be awarded

H and W, both in their late twenties, had been married $3\frac{1}{2}$ years. There were no children. W has obtained a divorce based on H's adultery. They both have successful careers so there is no question of maintenance, and neither of them is eligible for legal aid. The former matrimonial home, in which H is still living, was bought by him before the marriage with a mortgage of £10,000, the balance being paid from his own savings and from a legacy. The house is now worth £40,000 after deduction of the outstanding mortgage. Neither party has any other significant capital.

W brings proceedings for financial provision, claiming a lump sum of £15,000. H fights this on the basis that because of the length of the marriage and the fact that the purchase of the house was entirely financed by him, and that W has sufficient earnings to obtain a mortgage herself, she should receive, if anything, only a small lump sum. The matter proceeds to a hearing, at which the registrar makes an order in W's favour for a lump sum of £7,500. By now, they have run up legal fees of £1,500 (£750 each).

The alternatives in these circumstances are:

(i) W gets an order for party-and-party costs

	£		£
W gets		cost to H	
lump sum from H	7,500	lump sum to W	7,500
less: own legal fees	750	own legal fees	750
		party/party costs of W	600
	6,750		8,850
add party/party costs			
paid by H	600		
W gets	7,350		

(ii) W gets order for half costs

It is possible that because W has run up unnecessary costs in fighting the action, the registrar feels that she is not entitled to all her party-and-party costs, and makes an order for half her costs to be paid by H. The effect of this in the above example is that W would end up getting £7,050 with the cost to H being £8,550.

(iii) H's solicitor makes a 'Calderbank' offer

To protect H from having to pay two lots of costs as well as a lump sum, his solicitor wrote at some stage a 'without prejudice' letter, making an offer of a settlement of £9,000 in all. Because the offer was 'without prejudice' it was privileged and could not be revealed to the registrar without the consent of both parties.

The letter, however, went on to say that the offeror reserved the right to bring the letter to the court's attention on the question of costs at the conclusion of the case. Since W did not accept and went ahead with her claim for £15,000, she has to pay H's party-and-party costs from the date of the offer to the hearing. H, however, has been ordered to pay her costs only up to the date of the offer.

At the stage when H wrote the letter offering £9,000 in settlement, the parties' costs were only £250 each. If W had accepted, the position would have been

	£		£
W would have got		cost to H	
lump sum from H	9,000	lump sum to W	9,000
less: own costs	250	own costs	250
	———	W's party/party	
	8,750	costs	200
add party/party			———
costs payable by H	200		9,450
	———		
	8,950		

Since W refused and pressed on with the claim (getting an order for a lump sum of £7,500), costs on both sides have now run up to £750 each. The position is now as follows:

	£		£
W gets		cost to H	
lump sum from H	7,500	lump sum to W	7,500
less: her own legal fees	750	own costs	750
H's party/party costs		W's party/party costs to	
since the offer	400	date of offer	200
	———		———
	6,350		8,450
add own party/party costs		*less:* own party/	
before date of offer		party costs after	
payable by H	200	offer, payable by W	400
	———		———
	6,550		8,050

H has substantially improved his position on costs by making a realistic offer at an early stage. W, by not accepting the 'Calderbank' offer, has gambled away £2,400 – the difference between what she would have got if she had settled and what she eventually got in pursuit of another £6,000 (the difference between what she was offered in settlement and what she was originally claiming). H, as it happens, pitched his offer about right, and saved himself £1,400 in the process.

However, 'Calderbank' will be a lottery unless you or your solicitor can accurately forecast what order the court is likely to award and unless the build-up of the costs has been properly monitored. It is part of the job of an experienced divorce lawyer to keep in touch with the level of awards being made by the courts and especially with the kind of awards usually made by the local registrars.

In the example, the parties were at least fighting over an asset of some substance, but supposing that instead of the house being worth £40,000, it had been worth only £20,000, and the wife's initial claim was for £7,000, it is unlikely that the costs on both sides would have been significantly lower, so that the percentage impact of the costs consequences of a Calderbank offer would be even greater.

when costs are paid

The theoretical (and usually the practical) position is that the successful party has to pay his or her own solicitor's costs first and then recover the contribution ordered by the court from the other party. Usually, the solicitor will continue to act by preparing the bill and having it taxed and enforced against the payer.

Sometimes the solicitor may not press his client for payment of that part of his costs which are recoverable against the paying party but that is entirely a matter of the solicitor's benevolence and his assessment of the prospect of the other side paying up.

Change in circumstances

A lump sum or property adjustment order, once made, cannot be varied nor can you go back to court to obtain another one. With a periodical payments order, however, even if a spouse has merely a nominal order of, say, 5 pence per year, it would be possible to apply to the court to have the order varied if it can be shown that the financial circumstances of either party have changed.

Whenever there is a material change of circumstances, it is open to either of the couple to go back to the court and apply for the existing order for maintenance to be varied – that is, for the amount payable to be increased or decreased, or even for the order to be brought to an end.

An application for a variation can be made at any time on or after the decree nisi, even many years later provided that the recipient has not married again. There is no limit on the variations that can be applied for.

The court can also vary any agreement that the couple had made between themselves, even though they may have agreed not to refer the agreement to the court. In law, any agreement that precludes one party from seeking the assistance of the courts is void.

Although a lump sum order cannot be varied, if the lump sum is being paid in instalments, the size and frequency of instalments can be varied, but not so as to alter the total of the lump sum originally awarded.

If no maintenance order was made at the time of the divorce, either party can apply for an order at any time later. But leave of the court for the petitioner to make the application will be necessary if a request for maintenance had not been included in the petition.

If an application for maintenance made previously was formally dismissed by the court with the consent of the applicant, the application cannot be revived later.

applying for a variation

An application can be made at the divorce court where the order you want to vary was made. If that original court is now inconvenient, you can ask for the case to be transferred to one more convenient for you. (If the order was registered in a magistrates' court, that is the court to which you must apply.)

The application should be made on the standard form of notice of application available from the court office, supported by an affidavit with up-to-date details of your financial position, and of the change in circumstances giving rise to the application. The procedure is the same as for the first application for ancillary relief. Any variation can be back-dated to the date of the application.

If the court rejects the application for a variation, this does not preclude an application for a variation being made at some later stage if circumstances change again.

The original legal aid certificate will not cover the solicitor's work done in connection with an application for a variation; a new one would have to be applied for.

reasons for an application

Major events that are likely to affect any financial orders made in the divorce court are

● a change in financial circumstances of the payer or payee, including retirement

● remarriage of the payee (periodical payments order ends)

● remarriage of the payer

● death of either

● either party becoming disabled

● children getting older (index-linking of maintenance payments for children is rare – and might have the effect of inhibiting an application for an increase in payments that would otherwise be justified by the children becoming older or the father getting richer).

marriage of spouse

On remarriage, a former wife's right to maintenance ceases immediately and cannot be revived against that ex-husband even if she again be divorced or if her second husband dies.

There is no formal requirement to tell the previous husband that she has married again, but if she does not do so and he finds out, he can ask her to repay what he has paid her since her new marriage; if she does not pay up, he can sue her for the overpaid money as a debt.

Maintenance payments to or for children are not automatically affected by the mother's new marriage, but the remarriage of either parent may give rise to a situation in which a variation is justified (such as the paying parent's new commitments).

An ex-wife's right to occupy what had been the matrimonial home may cease on remarriage; the terms of the court order may require the house now to be sold and the proceeds divided in the specified proportions.

If you made a lump sum payment of, say, £10,000 to your ex-spouse and two months later you hear that she or he has remarried, you cannot apply for a variation. (In rare cases, an application to have the order set aside on the grounds of fraud may succeed.) And if a lump sum has been ordered to be paid in instalments and the recipient ex-spouse marries again, instalments have to be continued until the full amount is paid.

cohabitation

If you are paying your ex-spouse maintenance and she cohabits with someone else, you may have grounds to apply to the court for a variation of the order. The court will normally expect it to be proved that there is some permanence to the cohabitation and that it is reasonable to infer that there is financial contribution from the cohabitant.

If you are paying maintenance to your ex-spouse and children and you set up home with someone who already has children, which involves you in additional expense, this does not mean that your obligations to your former spouse and children cease. It may, however, provide you with grounds for variation. The court will take into account your new obligations even if you are not married, but these will normally be expected to take second place to your obligations to the children of your first marriage.

retirement

In the case of either the payee or the payer's retirement, an application should be made to vary the order by the party who is feeling the pinch. In these circumstances, the one-third formula will almost certainly never be applied. Usually, the court is just concerned to share out the more limited finances fairly.

death of former spouse

When the recipient dies, the payer can immediately stop any maintenance payments. But any outstanding instalments of a lump sum become due to the deceased's estate, and an unfulfilled transfer of property order can be enforced by the estate.

If the person paying maintenance dies, the maintenance order comes to an end (unless the order was for secured payments). The former spouse may be able to apply to the court under the Inheritance (Provision for Family and Dependants) Act 1975 for financial provision out of the deceased's estate (unless the court had previously granted an application that such a claim shall not be made). An application can also be made by or on behalf of a child. The application should be made within six months of the death.

life insurance

Because maintenance payments will cease when the payer dies, it may be advisable on divorce for the spouse who is going to be dependent on payments from the other to take out a life insurance policy on the payer's life. And the parent who does not have care and control of the children may want to take out an insurance policy on the life of the parent who is looking after the children, so that if the custodial parent were to die while the children are still dependent, some money would become available towards the extra cost to the other parent of then taking on responsibility for the children.

The policy could be a whole-life policy where the sum assured is paid out whenever the person dies or a 'term' insurance which pays out a set sum on death within so-many years, taken out for the period of likely dependence (premiums for term policies are generally lower than for other types of life insurance). There are some term insurance policies, called 'family income benefit' policies, where instead of one lump sum on the insured person's death, regular sums are paid (say, every quarter) for the balance of the insured period.

other help on death

On the death of her former husband, a divorced woman may get a 'child's special allowance' from the DHSS for any child in her family whom he had been maintaining. She can apply for this allowance on form CSI, available from any social security office.

Occupational pension schemes normally provide a lump sum death benefit (of up to four times the member's pay) if the member of the scheme dies before retirement. After the divorce, it is likely that the ex-husband will have changed the name of the person he wishes to receive the money on his death, so that his ex-wife may not benefit. The decision whether to pay any sum to her would, however, ultimately rest with the trustees of the pension scheme.

a will

A will made by either husband or wife is not automatically revoked on divorce, but the will is interpreted as if the ex-spouse had died on the day before the divorce: any gift left to him or her will go to whoever is entitled to the residue of the estate. If the ex-spouse is named as executor, that appointment will be of no effect.

In Northern Ireland and Scotland, a will is not affected by divorce.

If there is no will and a divorced person's estate has to be dealt with under the intestacy rules, his or her former spouse will not be taken into account in the distribution of the estate. But any children remain eligible for their share of an inheritance.

It is advisable to make a (new) will when divorce proceedings are started, in case you die before the decree absolute. But remember that if you marry again, marriage automatically revokes an earlier will (except in Scotland) unless it was made in contemplation of the marriage.

variation of a magistrates' court order

Magistrates' court orders also can be varied, either upward or downward, where there has been a change in circumstances, and they will cease automatically on death.

If the couple subsequently divorce, this will not necessarily bring a magistrates' court order to an end. It will end automatically only if the divorce county court substitutes its own order. If not, the magistrates' court order will continue, and also the right to apply for a variation. It will cease automatically on the payee's remarriage. If the payer remarries, this does not affect the order but may provide grounds for variation.

In the case of a lump sum, the position is different to that in divorce proceedings: there is apparently no restriction on the number of occasions on which a lump sum may be ordered (subject to the £500 limit each time).

registered order

If a divorce court order has been registered in the magistrates' court, application for a variation has to be made to the magistrates' court. The magistrates' court cannot discharge a divorce court order but can vary the amount of the order on application. No affidavits are required, and the magistrates will not have before them the information and calculations (for instance, about tax) on which the registrar at the divorce court based his original order. So, unless they are provided with full up-to-date information about the parties' finances, they may reduce the order unrealistically.

Enforcement of maintenance payments

Whatever the court orders, the actual payment of maintenance depends on the continuing willingness and ability of the ex-spouse to make the payments.

Should the payer (usually the ex-husband) fall into arrear with maintenance payments, there are several channels for enforcement, none entirely satisfactory. Whichever method is adopted, the sooner steps are taken to enforce the arrears, the better. If arrears are allowed to accumulate, they may well prove impossible to recover.

when on supplementary benefit

Registration of an order in the magistrates' court is useful when the amount of maintenance is equal to or less than the rate of any supplementary benefit entitlement. When the order is registered, the payments due under the order can be assigned by the woman to the DHSS who will then pay her the full amount of her supplementary benefit entitlement, irrespective of whether any payments are made by the man or not. This saves anxiety and inconvenience if he does not pay up.

Where the amount of the order is greater than the supplementary benefit entitlement, payments by the DHSS will be limited to the amount of supplementary benefit the woman is entitled to.

The DHSS can ask the woman if she agrees to take a case in the magistrates' court against the man to try and make him pay (called 'liable relative' proceedings). If she does not want to do this, the DHSS should not try to persuade her, but can take proceedings themselves to enforce the order that has been assigned to them.

The DHSS have a duty to the public to try to recover money they pay out on supplementary benefit from the person legally responsible for supporting the claimant. A man is not legally responsible for supporting and maintaining his ex-wife unless ordered by a court to pay maintenance to her. If he refuses to pay the due amount and the DHSS are satisfied that he has the means to pay, they can take him to court under 'liable relative' proceedings.

enforcing a debt

A defaulting spouse getting away with it is part of the wider problem of trying to enforce civil debts in general. Do not be too optimistic about your likelihood of success.

The main methods of enforcement are a warrant of execution, an attachment of earnings order, or a judgment summons.

warrant of execution

A warrant of execution is an order issued by the county court for the district where the defaulting payer lives, for the court bailiff to seize sufficient of the person's goods as will on sale by auction discharge the debt shown on the warrant.

Secondhand goods seized and sold at auction rarely produce much money. It is only worthwhile to get a warrant of execution if the goods are in good condition – but the threat of seizure and sale may produce payment.

To get a warrant issued, you must swear an affidavit showing the amount of the arrears, provide a copy of the order, complete the appropriate county court forms and pay the fee (which is 15p per £ of the amount of the warrant, minimum fee £5; not returnable if there are no saleable goods).

attachment of earnings order

Provided that the ex-husband is in regular employment, an attachment of earnings order may be a more effective way of collecting arrears. It requires the employers to deduct regular weekly or monthly amounts from his wages and to send them to the court who will then pay them to the woman. The amount of deductions can include not only a regular sum off the arrears until they are discharged, but also the ongoing maintenance. (The employers can deduct 50p in addition each time for their pains.) The procedure is no use where the man is unemployed or self-employed.

The application has to be to the divorce county court which made the maintenance order. The appropriate application form (in duplicate) with a copy of the maintenance order, must be supported by an affidavit giving details of the arrears and, if possible, the name of the employers. The court fee for an application is 10p per £ of the amount claimed (minimum fee £5).

A notice of the application is served on the ex-husband, together with a form asking for details of his income and commitments. The court can ask the employers to supply information about the man's earnings over the past few weeks.

protected earnings
Any order made will be on the basis that it must not reduce the man's net income below the protected earnings rate. This is the amount which would be allowed him and his dependants for supplementary benefit, together with the amount of his rent (or mortgage) and rates and other essential and reasonably long-term commitments, such as other court orders or a hire purchase agreement.

Where the protected earnings rate comes to considerably less than the order for maintenance, the payer can apply to the registrar to reduce the original maintenance order at the same time.

if registered
If the order for maintenance has been registered in the magistrates' court, an attachment of earnings order can be made by the magistrates provided payment is 4 weeks in arrear.

judgment summons

A judgment summons can be issued for maintenance arrears. If it can be shown that the ex-husband has the means to pay maintenance and has failed to do so, in theory he can be sent to prison. A judgment summons is a potentially effective means of enforcing payment of arrears, where a man has capital or is self-employed and cannot be touched by an attachment of earnings order.

A request for a judgment summons can be made to any divorce county court convenient to the applicant. Legal aid is not available for a judgment summons in the county court but is in the High Court. If the applicant would be eligible, the solicitor should apply to have the case transferred to the High Court.

The woman, or her solicitor, should attend the hearing of the judgment summons, in order to question the ex-husband in an endeavour to prove that he could have paid the maintenance but neglected to do so. If it is proved that he had the means, an order committing him to prison can be made. Sending him to prison is unlikely to produce the money that the ex-wife needs – although the threat of imprisonment may do so. The order can be suspended if he undertakes to pay regular amounts off the arrears together with current maintenance payments; it can be reinstated if he fails to keep up the payments.

The court is likely to order the erring ex-husband to pay the costs of the application and this can be a salutary lesson to him.

disappearing ex-husband

If the woman does not know her ex-husband's address, it may be possible to get the DHSS to disclose it to the court because his up-to-date address may be known to them through his national insurance records. A form can be obtained from the court on which the ex-wife should give as much information as she can about his last known address and employer and national insurance number.

The ex-husband's address will not be given to the ex-wife, either by the DHSS or the court.

enforcement of lump sum or property transfer order

An unpaid lump sum may be enforced either by bankruptcy proceedings (unwise) or by a court order that any property belonging to the person ordered to pay be sold to raise the sum. An order for such a sale (for example, of a house or stocks and shares) can be asked for when the lump sum is ordered or at any time thereafter.

If a transfer of property order is not complied with, the registrar at the court can execute the relevant conveyance in place of the person who is refusing to do so. Application has to be made to the court with the relevant documents prepared for the registrar and an affidavit in support.

It is advisable to have a solicitor's help for such enforcement proceedings.

Where to turn

when	go to	for	provided that	effective
marriage breaking up	conciliation service solicitor	discussion advice (£5 fixed-fee interview)	partner comes too	straightaway
spouse violent to self or children	magistrates' court	exclusion or protection order	still married and living together and threat of further violence	from date of order
	county court	ouster or non-molestation injunction		from date of order
spouse not providing (enough) money	magistrates' court	order for maintenance and/or lump sum (up to £500)	still married, can prove neglect to maintain	from date of order
	county court	order for maintenance and/or lump sum	can prove neglect to maintain, or divorce petition filed	from date on order
	DHSS	supplementary benefit	resources below set limits; not in full-time work	when assessment completed
		or		
		family income supplement	earnings below set limit; at least one child	when assessment completed (lasts for one year)

agreement reached to pay maintenance	magistrates' court	agreed maintenance order	still married	from date of order
	divorce county court	consent order	divorce petition filed	from date on order
wanting maintenance	divorce county court	maintenance pending suit	divorce petition filed	from date on order until decree absolute
		or periodical payments order		from decree absolute
non-owning spouse wanting to protect right to occupy home	Land Registry (registered property)	registration of a notice	still married to owning spouse	from date of registration until decree absolute
	Land Charges Registry (unregistered property)	registration of a class F land charge	still married to owning spouse	from date of registration until decree absolute

when	go to	for	provided that	effective
decision needed re matrimonial home (e.g. who is to live there, how to divide proceeds)	divorce county court	property adjustment order	divorce petition filed, applicant not married again	from decree absolute
decision needed re division of family assets	county court	settlement of ownership	still married or less than 3 years since divorce	straightaway
	divorce county court	property adjustment order lump sum order	divorce petition filed, applicant not married again	from decree absolute
ex-spouse failing to make periodical payments as ordered	magistrates' court	enforcement	order registered there and you know where he is	straightaway
	divorce county court	judgment summons	that court issued original order	from date of summons, warrant or order

		or warrant of execution or attachment of earnings order		
DHSS		supplementary benefit or family income supplement	resources below set limits; not in full-time work	when assessment completed
			earnings below set limit; at least one child	when assessment completed (lasts for one year)
wanting change in amount of maintenance being paid	court where original order made or magistrates' court where order registered	variation order	significant change in circumstances, payee not married again	from date on order

Three couples

Three fictitious couples, at various stages of their marriages, illustrate the different financial effects that divorce would bring, depending on commitments, children, jobs and the couples' respective ages. (The reason why the marriage has broken down will affect the financial results only in exceptional cases.)

You and your partner will not fit exactly into these three examples, but you should be able to identify sufficiently with one of the models to estimate your own likely financial problems and judge whether it would be possible to divorce on a financially reasonable basis.

Housing costs represent 25% to 30% of total household expenditure. It is therefore obvious that two homes out of one salary cuts down considerably what is left for food, clothing and other expenses. The money there is will have to go further and you both need to be better at budgeting than ever before.

If you feel that you would find the advice of a lawyer reassuring, be sure to present the lawyer at the first interview with all your financial details and as much as are known of your partner's. It will greatly speed up the case if you and your solicitor have a complete financial picture at the beginning. This information is all too often made available at too late a stage, when costs have been incurred, even though there was only one likely solution in the first place, and the matter should have been settled months previously.

You may be divorcing your spouse, but you cannot divorce your children; you are still a parent and as such will want any money available to go to them and not on unnecessary legal costs.

Couple 1 – Stewart and Liza

Stewart, aged 25, a graduate in computer studies, marries Liza, a teacher aged 22. She gets a probationary first post and they rent a flat to be near to her school and also convenient for Stewart who goes to his job by train. They save quite hard and pool their earnings in a joint building society account. After two years they buy a small house in their joint names, with the assistance of a 85% mortgage. They continue working and generally bring the house up to a good state of repair, sharing the work equally.

STAGE I

ages:	Stewart 28, Liza 25
number and ages of children:	none
length of marriage:	3 years (at the time, minimum period for divorce)
matrimonial home:	owner-occupied; 2 bed semi
equity (i.e. if sold, the difference between sale price and amount owing on mortgage)	£5,000
employment/income:	both in work: Stewart earning £8,000; Liza earning £7,000

What happens if they divorce now?

No obvious problem here, there are a number of choices.

the home

• The house could be sold and the proceeds split equally between them. This may give each of them enough for a deposit to buy something else. (The costs on one sale and two purchases would be high – solicitors, surveyors, estate agents, stamp duty if applicable, removals.)

• Stewart could raise the money (perhaps by increasing the mortgage) to buy Liza's half-share (£2,500) for her to put down as a deposit on another, cheaper, property. A problem would be if the value of the house had not risen sufficiently for the building society to lend Stewart a further £2,500, in which case he could perhaps ask his bank or employer for a loan.

• Liza could find a friend to share with (perhaps a colleague from her school) and they could together 'buy out' Stewart. Building societies have no objections in principle to giving a mortgage to two single people – they are only concerned with ability to repay.

If Stewart is buying out Liza, it will be necessary for Liza to surrender her interest in the property and transfer the legal title, and be released from her personal covenants on the mortgage. And vice versa if Liza buys out Stewart.

maintenance

Both are working and independent, so it would not be appropriate for either to be ordered to make maintenance payments to the other, and the couple can be independent of each other in the future. It is important to ensure that any claims made by either of them in the petition or answer are formally dismissed by the court so that they cannot be revived in the future.

Even if Stewart's income were, say, £15,000 compared to Liza's £7,000, he would not be ordered to pay her anything if the one-third formula were applied. Only if she was not working might he be required to make maintenance payments, and then they would almost certainly be limited to, say, two years.

STAGE II

The couple did not divorce after three years of marriage, but in their fourth year of marriage. They have a baby (John) and Liza has decided not to return to teaching for some time.

ages:	Stewart 29, Liza 26
number and ages of children:	one child, under 1 year old
length of marriage:	4 years
matrimonial home:	owner-occupied, 2 bed semi
equity:	£6,000
employment/income:	Stewart earning £9,750 shortly to be given a company car; Liza not working, receiving child benefit

What happens if they divorce now?

The existence of the child changes the whole picture.

the home

The child has to have somewhere to live. Usually, the most convenient place is the former matrimonial home and whoever has the child on a day-to-day basis ('care and control') will be able to remain in the home with the baby.

Liza has already given up her job to stay at home and take care of the baby and the court will not expect her to return to work for many years, if she does not wish to do so.

postponing sale

It is likely that the court will order that the house should not be sold until the child reaches 17 (or later if there is continued schooling or further education) and the proceeds then split between them. Meanwhile, Stewart will have to house himself elsewhere, without getting any capital out of the home and with a large part of his salary committed to Liza and the child.

The court is likely to transfer more of the equity in the house to Liza because

★ she will be responsible for some 17 years for paying off the mortgage
★ she will be responsible for maintaining the house
★ her future earning (and therefore mortgage) capacity will be substantially less than Stewart's
★ when the house is to be sold, Liza will need accommodation and her financial capacity will probably be limited
★ Stewart will in all probability have acquired a new home and will not have the same need for capital.

Stewart may wish to have a clause in the court order stating that should Liza marry or cohabit, the house should be sold forthwith. The court would be reluctant to agree to this although it might say that in these events he has the right to apply to the court for a sale.

Alternatively, the house may be transferred to the wife subject to a charge to the husband for about a third of the equity, enforceable on the child attaining the age of majority and thereafter ceasing full-time education, with liberty for him to apply to enforce the charge if the wife cohabits or remarries. (If she has to borrow money to pay off the charge, there would be no tax relief on the loan.)

The enforcement of the charge might be deferred for Liza's life or until she voluntarily vacates the home or remarries, particularly if Stewart's job prospects are better than normal.

If Liza wants later to move in order to buy an alternative house, Stewart's continued interest in the next house would need to be acknowledged. The new house would have to be bought on the same conditions as to sale or enforcement of the charge as before.

maintenance

There is only one salary, Stewart's, which after deducting national insurance and pension contributions comes to £9,000. Using the 'one-third' formula as a starting point would allocate to Liza an income of £3,000 per annum. (He would have to pay less than that if the child benefit she gets were counted in.) £3,000 is unlikely to be sufficient to pay the mortgage and the bills. Maintenance would be awarded to the baby, perhaps equal to the National Foster Care Association's recommended rates, which would come to about £1,250 p.a., and Liza would have that in full. But Stewart would be left with approximately £5,300 which is an insufficient income to live on and raise a moderate mortgage.

So, although stage II is only one year later than stage I, because of the child there is now little choice at all. Stewart and Liza must accept that they are both going to have to struggle financially and that legal arguments will not alter that position.

Liza will need enough money to keep the home going (gas, electricity, rates, insurance) and to pay the mortgage, and other outgoings.

Stewart will need enough money to keep up the maintenance payments, to pay for his own accommodation (whether renting or buying) and for his day-to-day expenses. Initially, he may also need to buy some household goods, and furniture.

From a tax point of view, the orders should be expressed to make the most of the tax allowances. By paying £500 p.a. more to the child (to make his payments £1,750 p.a.) instead of to Liza, she and John would effectively receive more without affecting the amount of total maintenance payments Stewart has to make.

Even so, Liza is not going to have enough for her needs and the baby's and must see how her resources might be increased.

help from the state

Liza can claim housing benefit from the local authority. The housing benefit scheme is available to owner-occupiers for rates (as well as to tenants for rent and rates).

After divorce, or 13 weeks after separating from her husband, the child benefit she gets will be increased by the one-parent benefit (at present £4.05 a week, tax free).

While she is not working, she may be eligible for supplementary benefit. If she goes back to work, she may be eligible for family income supplement which is available to a lone parent who is working for 24 hours a week or more.

Child benefit and one-parent benefit and any maintenance she receives will be taken into account in full when the DHSS works out her entitlement to supplementary benefit, or the local authority her housing benefit (a housing benefit supplement is available to help with housing costs for someone just over the limit for ordinary supplementary benefit).

maintenance ordered and supplementary benefit
If there is a likelihood that the proposed maintenance would bring her just above the level which would enable her to claim supplementary benefit, it may be of more practical use for her (and at the same time relieve Stewart of some expenditure) if the maintenance order were for slightly less so that, when assessed by the DHSS, her income would entitle her to supplementary benefit.

STAGE III

Liza and Stewart continue with their marriage and have a second child (Penny) in their sixth year of marriage. Stewart does well in his job and receives substantial promotion. They move in the following year to a new three-bedroomed detached house bought for £36,500 with a £25,000 20 year endowment mortgage (which means the amount borrowed does not reduce as time goes by).

After a further three years, when the children are aged 6 and 4, Liza returns to part-time teaching. Two years later, however, they get divorced. They agree to have joint custody of the children with 'care and control' to Liza. She is to remain in the house with the children and Stewart will leave.

ages:	Stewart 37, Liza 34
number and ages of children:	two; aged 8 and 6
length of marriage:	12 years
matrimonial home:	owner-occupied, 3 bed detached
equity:	£12,000
employment/income:	both in work: Stewart earning £17,000 plus company car; Liza's part-time earnings £6,000

What happens if they divorce now?

Still a problem, but not so difficult as at stage II.

Although there are now children and the mortgage payments are higher than at stage II, Stewart's increased salary and Liza's part-time earnings give the couple some freedom of manoeuvre. Their joint income after deducting national insurance and pension contributions is about £20,000 and one-third approximately £6,660. Liza's net income is about £5,770 (including child benefit of £6.50 a week per child), so Stewart would have to provide about £900 per annum for her and something for the children.

If the order for the children were based on the recommended rate for foster parents, John would get £30.45 per week (£1,583 p.a.) and Penny £27.79 per week (£1,445 p.a.). In view of his earnings, this is what the court might well order, as well as the £900 p.a. for Liza (so that his payments would come to a round £3,930 in all).

On the £900 p.a., Liza would have to pay tax at 30% (because her earnings use up her single person's tax allowance) but provided John and Penny's income is not in excess of their personal tax allowance of £2,005 p.a. each, no tax will be payable on what they get. So, from a tax point of view, the orders would be better expressed as a nominal payment for Liza of 5p p.a. (provided there is an order, even if it is only for a nominal amount, an application can be made at any time for a variation order to increase it if it is necessary) and to increase the orders for John and Penny. Their orders could be half of the £3,930 each (£1,965).

The £3,930 he is ordered to pay to Liza and the children is tax-deductible (in addition to his personal tax allowance of £2,005), so he will have to pay tax on £11,065 (£17,000 − £5,935). Liza, in addition to her personal tax allowance, would have the lone parent's additional personal allowance (APA) of £1,150.

Alternatively, to help with Liza's cash-flow problems, Stewart's order for each of the children could be made to fall within the small maintenance payments limit of £143 per month. This would come to £1,716 p.a. for each child (=£3,432), and the order for Liza could then be for £498 (£3,930 − £3,432), which should be expressed as £41.50 per month so as also to count as a small maintenance payment.

The net effect would be

for Stewart:	£	for Liza:	£
gross annual income:		*gross annual income:*	
earnings	17,000	earnings	6,000
		child benefit (+£4.05 p.w.)	887
		periodical payments	
		to children	3,432
		to self	498
			10,817
less:		*less:*	
tax at 30% on £11,065	3,320	tax at 30% on £3,343	1,003
national insurance	1,100	national insurance	540
pension contributions	1,020	pension contributions	360
payments to children	3,432	travel cost to work	240
payment to Liza	498		
available income	7,630	available income	8,674

(which is £636 per month plus use of car)   (which is £723 per month)

If the whole of the maintenance were paid to the children, with only the nominal 5p order to Liza, Stewart's available income would not be affected; Liza (and the children) would be about £12 per month better off, because she would be able to reclaim all the tax deducted from the maintenance payments.

the home

There is not sufficient money for them to sell this house and each to buy another. The parents both accept that the children are well settled in the present house. Liza teaches at the school the children attend, which is not far away, so they decide that she shall remain there with the children.

The mortgage will probably have to be changed to a repayment mortgage, in her name; Liza will have enough to pay the monthly repayments.

alternatives

● to leave the home in joint names, with a restriction that it is not to be sold until Penny reaches 17 or later if in full-time education (and that if Liza remarries or cohabits, Stewart should have the right to apply for a sale of the house). Stewart will therefore get his share in about 12 years' time. He could probably afford to borrow about £20,000 on mortgage, but the mortgagee might well not be too happy about this, bearing in mind his continuing liabilities to Liza. Liza, on the other hand, may not have enough to re-house herself when the home is finally sold unless she gets more than a half share of the proceeds because she had been carrying the mortgage repayments and upkeep of the house.

● to transfer the house to Liza but have her claim for periodical payments dismissed (so that she can make no future claims on Stewart) and pay a smaller amount of maintenance to the children. But this would not be a good thing for Stewart if Liza were to remarry (or cohabit) within the next 4 or 5 years, in which case she would have had to sell the house and share the proceeds with him and be no longer entitled to maintenance.

The advantage for Liza (although she would get less in the way of cash) would be that she could consider moving somewhere smaller and cheaper, to reduce her mortgage and outgoings, and she would not have to give up the house if she remarried.

Stewart, although losing a capital asset, would now be able to borrow on mortgage without too much difficulty. And he can push on in his career knowing that any substantial rises he may receive are his, and not to be drawn on for his ex-wife's maintenance (he may, however, still have to make increases from time to time to the children's maintenance).

STAGE IV

The couple's marriage survives until their silver wedding and then they split.

ages:	Stewart 50, Liza 46
number and ages of children:	two children aged 21 and 19; older child in hotel management away from home, younger child at university
length of marriage:	25 years
matrimonial home:	owner-occupied, 3 bed detached, with a few years of endowment mortgage still to run
equity:	£41,000
employment/income:	both in work: Stewart, director of finance, earning £30,000, plus company car; Liza, deputy headmistress, earning £11,000

What happens if they divorce now?

Almost as good a position as at stage I.

Stewart and Liza can lead financially independent lives because of their high salaries and the fact that the children are off their hands on a day-to-day basis, although each child will probably need money from time to time and an occasional home during vacations or holidays.

the home

The house is the three-bedroomed detached one bought new 18 years before. If they both want to sell it, after such a long marriage both would share the assets equally, and accordingly Stewart's share and Liza's share is £20,500 plus half the contents, plus half the profit on the surrender value of the endowment policy.

If Liza wishes to remain in the home, Stewart's capital in the home would be tied up until the mortgage is discharged in 2 years' time, unless she buys him out.

If Stewart wants the house to be sold and Liza does not, the court is likely to agree with him because the house is not now needed for the children.

maintenance

Stewart may want to make a covenant in favour of Penny while she is a student.

Liza might argue that she should receive some maintenance (£2,000 to £3,000 a year) from Stewart, because of his large salary. Whether this is ordered would depend on what is to happen about the house and contents.

The other factor that is relevant here is Liza's loss of pension rights under her husband's employers' scheme. Although she has rights to a retirement pension under her own scheme, she is losing out on a probably substantial lump sum and pension under Stewart's scheme, and at this age such a loss would be significant. So Stewart may be required to compensate her with a lump sum with which to buy a deferred annuity – again, depending on how they share their interests in the house.

Couple 2–Janet and Andy

Janet and Andy are a young couple, like many, whose incomes are not sufficiently high to offer any freedom of choice in financial arrangements on divorce.

Andy is 22, a recently qualified electrician. He meets Janet, a shorthand typist aged 19, at the firm where he works. They get married and go to live with Janet's parents in their 3-bedroomed council house. After 18 months, through hard saving and all their wedding present gifts of money, they buy a maisonette on a repayment mortgage. It is in an older house which has been converted and there is a great deal of modernisation to be done.

After about 15 months in their new home, in their third year of marriage, they have their first child (Zoe) and Janet gives up work, at least for a few months.

STAGE I

ages:	Andy 25, Janet 22
number and ages of children:	one, a few months old
length of marriage:	3 years
matrimonial home:	owner-occupied, 2 bed maisonette
equity (i.e. if sold, the difference between sale price and amount owing on mortgage)	£2,000
employment/income:	Andy earning £5,000 plus maximum £1,000 p.a. overtime; Janet not working, receiving child benefit; possibility of returning to work part-time at old job, if mother will look after the child.

What happens if they divorce now?

Problem: Andy's earnings are low and he is heavily committed.

the home

A home is necessary for the baby and Janet, and there is not enough money to re-house Andy.

Janet does not want to return with the baby to live with her mother, and would like to be allowed to remain in the maisonette until the child leaves school. This would mean Andy having to return to his parents' home or possibly sharing a rented flat with friends. It would be impossible for Andy on his earnings to pay Janet sufficient money for the mortgage repayments, the rates and other bills and to pay something for the baby.

If it is feasible for Janet to live with her parents and the alternative is to render Andy impoverished, the court may order the sale of the maisonette.

maintenance

In the past, Andy has taken on all the overtime going, but he may now feel that he is not prepared to do this. No court can force him to do overtime, but will assess him on what he has been doing and what it is reasonable for him to do (i.e. continue to earn some overtime). On the basis of an income of £5,000 (no overtime worked), giving one-third to Janet and, say, £7.50 per week to the child, would reduce Andy to below subsistence level. The court will always try to ensure that a man's income is above subsistence level.

Subject to there being no mortgage arrears, the court may order that Janet stays in the maisonette, gets no maintenance for herself (claim dismissed) and a small amount of maintenance (say, £8 a week) for the baby. She could then claim supplementary benefit, which would take care of the interest part of the mortgage payments and would get her housing benefit for the rates. She could work part-time, if her mother is available to baby-sit.

Janet will continue to receive child benefit and can also now claim one-parent benefit (a weekly addition of £4.05).

STAGE II

The couple survive the traumas of renovating the maisonette and having their first baby, and stay together. In their fifth year of marriage, they have a second baby (Quentin) and four years later when the children are 6 and 4, they move to a mid-terrace house which they buy jointly for £22,000, borrowing £17,000 on a repayment mortgage. They made a good profit on the sale of the maisonette and can therefore furnish the house, buy a 3-year old car, and have a little money behind them.

In their 12th year of marriage, they divorce.

ages:	Andy 34, Janet 31
number and ages of children:	two, Zoe aged 9 and Quentin 7
length of marriage:	12 years
matrimonial home:	owner-occupied, 3 bed terrace house
equity:	£14,000
employment/income:	both in work: Andy, now foreman electrician, earning £8,000; Janet working 9 to 4 as a secretary, earning £4,250

What happens if they divorce now?

The home is not sufficient to provide enough money for Andy and Janet to re-house themselves.

the home and maintenance

The children will be entitled to remain in the house for at least the next 10 years with whoever has 'care and control' of them.

If it is Janet who has left home to go to live with someone else, Andy may wish to have responsibility for the children and stay with them in the home. The court would not order a sale of the home until, at the very earliest, the children had left school. He has either to buy her out by paying her £7,000 now (provided he can raise the money, perhaps by increasing the mortgage) or, when the house is eventually sold, share the proceeds of sale with her—probably receiving more than half because of his maintaining the children, the mortgage and the home.

In these circumstances, it is unlikely that he would be required to pay any maintenance to Janet.

If it is Janet who stays and Andy goes, he will have to provide maintenance for the two children (but, on a one-third basis, not for her). Her income, if the maintenance to the children is included, will be sufficient to make the mortgage repayments.

Andy's remaining income could support perhaps a small mortgage but he has to declare to the building society that he is paying maintenance which reduces his available income, and he has no ready deposit. Although he is entitled to his share in the equity of the house, Janet cannot afford to buy him out at this stage.

At this stage, a divorce is pretty disastrous for Andy, and his standard of living will be much reduced. Janet, although superficially in a similar position as before the divorce, will find it very difficult to manage on the money. She will be under pressure to keep on her job, even if she feels that one or both of the children would be better off with more of her time. Moreover, she has to cope with the school holidays and the extra expenditure they entail.

If they sold the house, each of them would get less than £7,000 after conveyancing and estate agent's fees and neither would then be able to raise a large enough mortgage to buy something else.

Calculations at this stage

Janet and Andy's house is now worth £30,000 and they still owe £16,000 on mortgage. The equity is therefore £14,000.

They have no other assets of significant resale value.

gross monthly income

$$\text{Andy } £\left(8{,}000 \times \frac{1}{12}\right) = £667$$

$$\text{Janet } £\left(4250 \times \frac{1}{12}\right) = £354$$

Child benefit *(although her income, is not being counted in for calculating the starting point of her maintenance):* $\left(\dfrac{6.50 + 6.50 + 4.05}{12} \times 52\right) = £74$

unavoidable monthly outgoings

mortgage payment at 11.25% interest	£131.32
HP repayment and TV rental	£35.00
rates, water charges, gas/electricity, telephone (say)	£78.60
	£244.92

one-third calculation

	£	£
Andy		
gross monthly pay		667
less:		
national insurance	60	
travel costs to work	20	80
		587 (A)
Janet		
gross monthly pay		354
less:		
national insurance	32	
travel costs to work	20	52
		302 (B)
Total combined income (A + B)		889
divided by 3		296
less (B)		302
one-third starting point		−6

Therefore NIL maintenance for Janet

Maintenance for Quentin £75 p.m = £900 p.a.
          for Zoe £75 p.m = £900 p.a.

tax calculations

Andy	£	£	*Janet*	£
gross annual income:			gross annual income:	
earnings		8000	earnings	4250
less:			*less:*	
periodical payments			personal tax allowance	
to children	1800		(single person's plus APA)	3155
single person's tax				
allowance	2005			
		3805		
Taxable income		4195	Taxable income	1095
Tax on £4195 at 30% = £1259			Tax on £1095 at 30% = £329	

There will be no tax on the periodical payments to the children because neither payment is over £2005 p.a.

the 'net effect' calculations

Andy	£	£	*Janet*	£	£
gross monthly			gross monthly		
income:			income:		
earnings		667	earnings		354
			child benefit		74
			periodical		
			payments to		
			children		150
					578
less:			*less:*		
tax	105		tax	28	
national insurance	60		national insurance	32	
periodical					
payments to					
children	150				
travel costs to work	20	335	travel costs to work	20	80
Available monthly		332	Available monthly		498
income			income		

Although Janet will not exactly be rolling in money, she should be able to afford the mortgage payments for the house. Janet may be slightly worried about making ends meet. However, if she were to lose her job and had to claim supplementary benefit, she would get her mortgage interest paid by the DHSS.

STAGE III

Although Andy and Janet seriously considered divorcing at stage II, they decided they could not afford to and also thought it would disrupt the children's life too much. Accordingly, they stay together for another ten years.

ages:	Andy 44, Janet 41
number and ages of children:	two, aged 19 and 17, both working; the younger undergoing training, attending a college one day and one evening per week
length of marriage:	22 years
matrimonial home:	owner-occupied, 3 bed terrace house
equity:	£24,000
employment/income:	Andy, still foreman, now earning £10,000. Janet, now full-time secretary, about to be promoted to run a small office as manageress at a salary of £7,500.

What happens if they divorce now?

Still not quite enough money for two homes: a problem if court decides home should not be sold for a few more years.

maintenance

Andy will not be ordered to pay maintenance to the older child, Zoe, but he may consent to do so in the case of Quentin, the younger child who, although not in full-time education, is still training.

Janet's income is above the basic one-third starting point so she is unlikely to be awarded anything.

the home

In view of the ages of the children, the matrimonial home could be sold and the equity split 50/50 between Andy and Janet. A sale and division would give them approximately £11,500 each after costs but this is not sufficient for each of them to buy a new home.

If one of them did not want to sell the house, it is possible that the court would not allow a sale for a few years until the younger child finishes his college course. Janet would pay the mortgage, but Andy, even though he does not contribute, does not lose his right to a share in the equity when the house is finally sold. But this may be slightly less than 50% if the capital part of Janet's mortgage payments since the divorce are taken into account.

Another possible solution is for one of them to buy out the other. That would mean whichever of them stays in the house finding an extra £12,000 by increasing the mortgage. Although Janet could, just about, borrow £12,000 provided her job is secure, this would leave her very short of money on a day-to-day basis. But she could do whatever she likes with the house, such as take in lodgers, and when she sells it, perhaps to buy a cheaper one, the whole of the proceeds will be hers.

Janet or Andy may feel that something is to be gained from going to court. The approach to the court could be two-fold: to decide whether one party had good reason to continue living in the property to the exclusion of the other; secondly, to agree to increase the share of one party to the detriment of the other – say, 70/30 split of the proceeds.

The court will give consideration to each one's
★ contribution
★ needs
★ resources.

Both have contributed. One parent needs a house as a home or base for the children for a few more years. There are unequal resources. Subject to the risk of redundancy, Andy has a mortgage capacity of £18,000 or thereabouts. He would presumably need about £25,000 to £26,000 to buy a house for himself – less for a flat. He therefore needs £8,000 to £10,000 from the present house. Janet has a mortgage capacity of about £12,000 and her needs of accommodation remain as before. A transfer of the house to her on payment of £9,000 or £10,000 to him looks a likely solution.

Couple No. 3 – Kevin and Maureen

The third couple is also typical of many young people for whom if they divorce having had children, there is no choice at all about money. Going to court to try to negotiate a settlement is pointless because the result is inevitable.

At 17, Maureen is pregnant when she and Kevin, aged 20, decide to get married. Maureen recently left school and is unemployed. Both sets of parents offer a home to the couple but Maureen wishes to remain with her mother because of the baby. Kevin manages to keep employed on casual work throughout the summer, but is mainly out of work during the winter.

They have a second child in their third year of marriage. Having been on the waiting list for three years and now with two children, they are offered a two-bedroom flat by the council, which they accept. Two years later, they want to divorce. Kevin has had a few months of continuous work with his uncle, but this is likely to come to an end shortly.

STAGE I

ages:	Kevin 25, Maureen 22
number and ages of children:	two, aged 5 and 2
length of marriage:	5 years
matrimonial home:	council 2 bed flat in their joint names
employment/income:	Kevin presently employed as a casual labourer – almost certain to be unemployed soon; Maureen caring for children, never had a job

What happens if they divorce now?

Almost certainly both will be claiming social security for many years to come.

the home

Normally the home goes to the person who cares for the children, in this case Maureen. Kevin and Maureen's flat is in their joint names, so the court will order it to be transferred into Maureen's sole name.

The court can order the tenancy, even if it had been in Kevin's name only, to be transferred to Maureen, if she obtains custody. She cannot claim it 'as of right', neither can she expect to be allocated a property by the local authority once she moves out (unless she is forced to leave because Kevin is being violent and she has to be rehoused under the Housing (Homeless Persons) Act).

Kevin will either move in with someone else, or return to live with his parents.

maintenance

As Kevin works only infrequently and his present job is coming to an end, he is unlikely to be able to pay maintenance regularly to Maureen. But the court can make a periodical payments order for a minimum amount, so that this can be varied if the circumstances change. If Kevin is again in work, Maureen may feel it worthwhile to try for more maintenance because the court will not accept that Kevin can simply ignore his obligations to his ex-wife and children. She should ask for the increased order to be registered in a magistrates' court, so that she can apply to the DHSS to switch to supplementary benefit if he is not paying. If he is continually or partially unemployed, Maureen would be better off on supplementary benefit which will at least be a regular income.

It is rarely worthwhile pursuing the husband for maintenance because although the short-term rate of supplementary benefit is low, it is regular and after 12 months she automatically transfers to the long-term rate (which is considerably higher); she does not have to register for work while the children are under 16.

While Kevin is unemployed or in irregular work, nothing can alter Maureen's position, at whatever stage they divorce with whatever number of children. She may not even be able to get work later on as she has no particular training and there are fewer unskilled jobs available now.

Assuming that Maureen does not re-marry, she would need to be certain of obtaining significantly more maintenance than a sum which, after tax, provides her with long-term supplementary benefit rate, plus the amounts for two children plus rent and rates in full from housing benefit, and the exemptions that come with supplementary benefit. Altogether, this might come to nearly £90 a week for her.

The future possibilities are

● Kevin getting well-paid regular work and being able to pay a reasonable amount of maintenance (pretty unlikely)
or
● Maureen finding a job and continuing to get some maintenance from Kevin (also unlikely)
or
● Maureen remarrying or cohabiting (statistically a 1 : 2 chance of this).

There are many 'Kevins and Maureens' and in nearly every case the woman (custodial parent) can expect to be on supplementary benefit for many years, caught in the poverty trap.

Dealing with debts

When a couple has a joint bank or building society account on which cheques can be drawn with either signature, there is the risk that the account could be cleared out without the other spouse knowing about it. To prevent this, the bank manager or building society should be told to change the arrangement so that cheques can be drawn only with both signatures.

money advice

There are financial advice and debt counselling services in some areas, provided by voluntary organisations such as the CAB or by the local authority, primarily aimed at low-income families. Some have an appointment system, some are by referral from a CAB or other agency. These services are still relatively rare and local, and the picture is always changing. At present, there are money advice centres in

Birmingham: Birmingham Settlement, 318 Summer Lane; Voluntary Service Council, 161 Corporation Street

Brighton: Council for Voluntary Service, 17 Ditchling Rise

Gateshead: welfare rights section of social services department, Windmill Hills, Bensham Road

Leicester: 18 Friar Lane

London: Lambeth consumer services department, 138 Clapham Park Road, SW4 (Lambeth locals only); Mary Ward Financial Advice Centre, 42 Queen Square, WC1 (with legal advice centre)

Milton Keynes: Money Advice Service, 53 Wastel, Beanhill

Minehead: Community Information Bureau, The Lane Centre, Market House Lane

Newcastle upon Tyne: welfare rights section of social services department.

An increasing number of citizens advice bureaux provide advice and counselling specifically on debts and money problems. They may be able to work out a repayment schedule and help in negotiating with creditors. Areas where CAB offer specialist money advice include the

West Midlands, Gwent, West Glamorgan, West Yorkshire, Merseyside and parts of London. Generally the CAB is the place to go to first for help with a money problem; if there is a more appropriate centre locally, the bureau will tell you.

The Birmingham Settlement money advice centre has issued a *Self-help guide for debtors — a booklet for those who want to pay but can't*, which is available for 25p from the Money Advice Centre, 318 Summer Lane, Birmingham B19 3RL.

gas, electricity and telephone accounts

If you realise that there are arrears, straightaway call at the local showroom or contact the accounts department or area manager of the gas or electricity authority or the accounts division of your local telephone area, explain the situation, and ask not to be cut off. (The relevant addresses or telephone numbers are on the bills.) If payment is not made, the undertaking concerned has the right to cut off the supply.

There is a code of practice governing disconnection of gas and electricity, the effect of which is that supplies should not be cut off if you come to an agreement to pay off by instalments.

A leaflet on *How to get help if you can't pay your bill*, explaining the code of practice, is available from gas showrooms and electricity shops and CABx. If you come up against difficulties about arranging to pay off debts or making future payments, you should contact the area gas consumers' council or electricity consultative council, or get help from the citizens advice bureau or a consumer advice centre.

The gas or electricity authority and British Telecom may be prepared to enter into a fresh agreement with the wife who is left in the home and take steps against the husband for the unpaid bills. They may be entitled to make the wife pay off the arrears, perhaps by instalments, for the period she has been there on her own before accepting her as the new consumer, or insist on a security payment or deposit. Once the telephone has been cut off, there may be a charge for reconnection.

rates

If the husband was responsible for payment of the rates while the couple lived together in the home, he may go on being regarded as liable for the rates up to the decree absolute, even if he has left the home and notified the local authority. He could get sued for any arrears.

Failure to pay the rates can result in 'seizure by distress' by the local authority, who have the right to send the bailiff to take away the furniture, unless the spouse who lives there can claim it as being his or her own or can clear the arrears in a single payment or, if the local authority agrees, by instalments.

other debts

Generally, a wife or husband would be well advised to contact anyone to whom money is, or may be, owed as soon as possible after the breakdown of the marriage. Provided some reasonable proposals can be put forward, the creditors may prefer to come to some arrangement rather than rely on their legal rights and take the matter to court.

If you have offered the creditors to pay by instalments and they have not accepted, let them sue you. In the meantime, try to keep up the payments you have offered. If it comes to court, the court may order that payment be continued by the instalments unless the creditor can show that you can afford more.

It is a criminal offence to harass a debtor for payment of money: for example, a trader must not threaten to enter the premises to recover the goods. No creditor can enter your house without a court order to take away goods you have bought. Even then, the creditor himself cannot enter: the court order will be enforced by a county court official known as a bailiff (or in a High Court case, a sheriff's officer).

If the bailiff arrives at your door and your spouse, not you, is the debtor, none of your goods should be seized. If the bailiff will not accept that the goods are yours, you can make a written claim to the court and if the creditor does not accept that the goods are yours, the court will issue an 'interpleader' summons. You will have to provide such evidence as you have, by way of receipts, invoices, hire purchase documents, and you may have to attend court to prove your ownership.

If the debt is solely or jointly in your name, the bailiff will be entitled to seize your goods but you may apply to the court to stay execution, usually on the basis that you pay off the debts by instalments. The county court office will give you the necessary forms to complete.

The procedure in the High Court is more complicated and you may well need legal advice.

administration order

A debtor worried by creditors can apply to the county court for an administration order, provided there is at least one judgment debt against her or him (and the total debts are less than £5,000).

Under an administration order, the debtor pays into court, generally by weekly payments, a sum of money, decided by the court after taking into account the applicant's financial position. Out of the money paid in, the court will pay out sums of money periodically to the creditors. The court fee of 5p per £ has to be borne by the debtor: it is deducted before any money is distributed.

The burden is taken off you: all you have to do is to make sure that you pay in the ordered sum regularly.

Details of what is involved in an administration order can be obtained from county court offices and at citizens advice bureaux.

Debts in respect of rent, mortgage repayments, current HP payments, current gas and electricity bills, are usually excluded from administration orders.

drawback

An application for an administration order can be ill-advised if you own your house because it amounts to an act of bankruptcy. Although it is unusual for any creditors then to take bankruptcy proceedings, it is possible that they might, and that could lead to your being forced to leave the house.

hire purchase debts and similar commitments

The person who signed the hire purchase or credit sale agreement is responsible for payment. If the husband continues to pay the instalments, this could be taken into account by the divorce court in assessing the maintenance he has to pay to the wife or, conversely, if the wife pays the instalments.

An order can be obtained from the court transferring to one or other spouse the goods themselves once payments under the hire purchase agreement are completed.

If the husband gets into arrears, the wife has no say in any court proceedings taken by the finance company for return of the goods. However, the company may be prepared to reach an arrangement with her about payment of the money due to them, possibly by smaller instalments, or about terminating the agreement.

The finance company may claim the goods back – but if at least one-third of the price has been paid, a court order must be obtained and the procedure laid down in the Consumer Credit Act must be followed, before possession of the goods can be obtained.

Somebody receiving supplementary benefit may get help with HP commitments for essential furniture or household equipment through a weekly addition to the SB payment or perhaps through a single payment towards clearing the debt.

mortgage arrears

Where the husband has undertaken to continue the mortgage payments, the wife should ask the building society or other lender to keep her informed if he falls behind in the payments, to prevent substantial arrears arising unbeknown to her. Proceedings for possession may be instituted by the building society or other lender against the husband for possession of the house without the wife necessarily knowing about it. If she has registered a charge on the house to protect her right of occupation under the Matrimonial Homes Act, this would not protect where the mortgage is already in existence at the time of registration. But building societies are now statutorily required to give notice of any action for possession to a spouse who has registered her right of occupation.

As soon as she is aware of the building society's possession proceedings, the wife should get legal advice and apply to the court where the hearing is to be held and ask to be joined as a defendant. She could then counter the building society's claim on any ground that would be open to the husband and will have the opportunity to make out a case for saving the home. She is likely to succeed if she can show that it will be possible to pay off the arrears within a reasonable time – that means within one year, or at most two years.

As well as applying to the court, the wife should, urgently, speak directly to the relevant person at the building society who is concerned with the mortgage, and try to arrange some method of discharging the debt. She should also take steps to get the husband to fulfil his undertaking to make the mortgage payments. But if the wife can make the mortgage payments herself, she should do so: the building society must accept them.

privately rented property

Where the tenancy is in the name of the husband alone, he is liable for paying the rent. If the landlord starts possession proceedings against the husband because of non-payment of the rent, the wife should seek legal advice and apply to be joined as a defendant so that she can use any defence open to the husband under the Rent Acts or Housing Act. This includes the right to apply for the order to be suspended, on condition that she will pay off the arrears of rent by instalments.

The Matrimonial Homes Act gives the wife the right to live in the house or flat up to the date of the decreee absolute and provides that payment of the rent, or arrears of rent, by the wife must be accepted by the landlord. If she is to remain there, it is essential that the tenancy be transferred to her, preferably before the decree is made absolute. Notice of such an application under the Matrimonial Homes Act must be served on the husband and on the landlord, and they are entitled to be heard on the application.

An application for a transfer of property order in divorce proceedings does not need to be served on the landlord nor has he any right to be heard by the court.

threat of eviction

Before the worst comes to the worst and the wife is evicted, she should get in touch with the local authority (the housing department or the social services department). Under the Housing (Homeless Persons) Act 1977, the local authority have to take action whenever someone who is homeless or threatened with domestic violence or homelessness approaches them for help in relation to accommodation. This help may be advice only or an offer of temporary accommodation and then rehousing if in priority need – for example, if with children or vulnerable through ill health. A person with whom dependent children are living is considered as having a priority need.

Advice and help

Anyone in difficulties over finance, tax, housing, the children, or rights generally, can go for advice to a **citizens advice bureau**. CAB offices have numerous leaflets and information about local sources of help and services. The address of a local citizens advice bureau can be found in the telephone directory.

The Child Poverty Action Group (CPAG, 1 Macklin Street, London WC2B 5NH) has a citizens rights office (telephone: 01-405 5942) where guidance can be sought on financial matters and particularly benefit problems. CPAG publishes *The national benefits handbook* (£3 including postage) which covers supplementary benefit and other means-tested benefits. *The rights guide to non-means-tested social security benefits* (£3) covers other social security benefits. *The rights guide for home owners* (£1.50), co-published with SHAC, is aimed at home owners on a low budget.

The National Council for One Parent Families (255 Kentish Town Road, London NW5 2LX, telephone: 01-267 1361) works to help parents who are looking after children on their own. It issues various books, reports, pamphlets and leaflets on problems that a single parent may encounter, including on taxation, housing, social security benefits, divorce and children.

Gingerbread, a nationally organised self-help association (head-quarters at 35 Wellington Street, London WC2E 7BN, telephone: 01-240 0953), has about 350 local groups providing practical and supportive help and advice for single-parent families.

Families Need Fathers (37 Carden Road, London SE15 3UB, telephone: 01-639 5362) provides help and support for all non-custodial parents who are having problems over access or custody (not just fathers). FNF has local groups in various parts of the country, and issues a quarterly newsletter (free to members). It has published a booklet *Divorce and your child* (50p) and other booklets on problems encountered by parents apart from their children.

The National Family Conciliation Council (secretary at Llanberis, Brooklands Way, East Grinstead, West Sussex RH19 1DE) may be able to give you the address of an affiliated conciliation service in your area or near where you live.

Where problems arise over the home – mortgage, occupation of the home, rates, rent and other payments – advice is available from **Shelter** (157 Waterloo Road, London SE1 8XF, telephone: 01-633 9377, with centres in other towns), and from **SHAC** (London Housing Aid Centre, 189a Old Brompton Road, London SW5 0AR, telephone: 01-373 7276) dealing with the London boroughs only, or from a local housing aid or advice centre (addresses are listed in the telephone directory).

There are **legal advice centres** in various parts of the country where lawyers working voluntarily give legal advice free (only a limited amount, if any, of further assistance is given). The centres are open only at specified hours.

At **law centres**, full-time legal staff will handle a case from beginning to end, including representation at court. The service is generally free but restricted to clients who cannot afford to pay solicitors' fees. The Law Centres Federation (Duchess House, Warren Street, London NW1) can provide a list of law centres and information about their work (send a stamped addressed envelope). The Legal Action Group publishes a directory of legal advice and law centres and the local CAB or library should have a copy.

The **Department of Health and Social Security** administers most state benefits. The DHSS issues a pamphlet FB2, called *Which benefit?* (available at local social security offices), listing 60 ways in which you can get cash help in times of need. It gives current conditions and rates of payment, and refers to other sources of help and information and relevant DHSS leaflets. Leaflet FB3, *Help for one parent families*, gives details of benefits available for parents caring for children on their own. There are also leaflets on help with heating costs, how to claim various welfare services free, *Your retirement pension if you are divorced* (NP 32A) national insurance contribution rates (NI 208) and benefit rates (NI 196).

In all areas of the country except London postal districts, there is a Freefone service which gives general information, advice and guidance on social security benefits, and will send relevant leaflets and claim forms. To get put through, dial 100 and ask your operator for 'Freefone DHSS'.

GETTING AN UNDEFENDED DIVORCE BY SPECIAL PROCEDURE

	time stage	who acts	action required and documents involved
1	—	spouse wanting divorce	may go to solicitor for advice on grounds for divorce and for help with completing petition gets appropriate form of petition and, if relevant, statement as to arrangements for children, from divorce county court office
2	any time 3 years after date of marriage (after 1 year under new 1984 legislation)	petitioner (spouse wanting divorce)	lodges at court office: completed petition plus copy for spouse (and named co-respondent, if petition based on adultery) certified copy of marriage certificate two copies of completed statement as to arrangements for children, where relevant pays fee of £40 to court office (or completes form to get exemption of fee)
3	within a few days of (2) depending on the court's workload	court office	sends to other spouse (respondent) copy of petition, statement as to arrangements for children, notice of proceedings, and acknowledgment of service for completion (in adultery case, all documents except statement re children also sent to co-respondent, if named)
4	within 8 days of receiving documents in (3) (longer if respondent living outside England or Wales)	respondent (and co-respondent)	should return acknowledgment of service to court, plus, if appropriate, counter-proposals re arrangements for children

5a	if acknowledgment of service not returned	court office	notifies petitioner and gives information about alternative methods of service
b	once acknowledgment of service returned	court office	sends copy of acknowledgment of service to petitioner, plus form of request for directions for trial and form of appropriate affidavit in support of petition, to be completed
6	after 5b **or** after 29 days from service of petition (3), if respondent (or co-respondent) indicated intention to defend on acknowledgment of service but has not filed an answer	petitioner	i completes affidavit in support of petition, takes it to a solicitor or court for swearing, plus copy of acknowledgment of service, identifying respondent's signature thereon (or in adultery case, a confession statement from respondent) ii completes request for directions for trial (sent at stage **5** by court office) and takes/sends to court plus completed affidavit with any relevant supporting documents copy of any previous court orders relating to the marriage or the children
7	when request for directions for trial received	registrar	reads and considers the documents
8a	if all in order	i registrar	certifies entitlement to decree (and to any costs claimed, if appropriate) fixes date for pronouncement of decree by judge and for his consideration of arrangements re children
		ii court office	sends notification of date(s) to petitioner and respondent

time	stage	who acts	action required and documents involved
	b if registrar not satisfied	i registrar	requests further evidence or information
		ii petitioner	has to supply required evidence or information to court
		iii registrar	considers further evidence or information supplied
	if registrar then satisfied	iv court office	fixes date for pronouncement of decree by judge and for his consideration of arrangements re children
			sends notification of date(s) to petitioner and respondent
	c if registrar still not satisfied	i registrar	removes case from special procedure list
		ii court office	informs petitioner and respondent
	9 on date given in 8a(ii) or 8b(iv)	i judge	pronounces decree nisi (petitioner and respondent need not be present)
		ii court office	sends copy of decree to petitioner and respondent
	10 same day as 9 or on date given in 8a(ii) or 8b(iv)	parent(s)	parent with whom children will live must, the other parent may also, come before judge in chambers to answer questions about arrangements for the children
		judge	considers arrangements for children
	11a if satisfied: same day	judge	certifies satisfaction as to children and, where appropriate, makes order for custody/access
	b if not satisfied: same day	i judge	may order court welfare officer's report and/or further information from parents and/or refer for conciliation
		ii court office	fixes date for adjourned hearing and notifies parents
	c on date fixed in 11b(ii)	parent(s)	attend adjourned hearing before judge with the required additional information
		judge	re-considers arrangements, and, if satisfied, makes appropriate order(s) and certifies satisfaction

12	six weeks and one day after (9) (provided judge has certified satisfaction re children)	petitioner	applies to court (on form available from court office) for decree to be made absolute
13	when application in (12) received	court office	checks court records that no reason why decree should not be made absolute issues certificate making decree nisi absolute sends copy of decree absolute to ex-husband and ex-wife

OR

if petitioner has not applied at stage 12:

14a	after three months and six weeks since (9)	i respondent	may apply to have decree made absolute, with affidavit in support of application
		ii court office	fixes date for application to be heard; returns one copy of application to respondent
b	by not later than 4 days prior to date fixed for hearing at 14a(ii)	respondent	sends copy of application and notification of date to petitioner
15a	on date fixed at 14a(ii)	respondent	attends before registrar
		registrar	considers application
b	if registrar satisfied	court office	issues certificate making decree nisi absolute sends copy of decree absolute to ex-husband and ex-wife

Glossary

access
the right granted by the court to the parent with whom the child is not living for the child to visit that parent or stay with him or her for short periods

acknowledgment of service
form sent by the court to the respondent with the petition, with questions about his or her intentions and wishes in response to the petition; its return to the court establishes service of the petition

administration order
an arrangement for a debtor faced with a number of debts and with at least one judgment against him, whereby he makes regular fixed payments into court; the court redistributes these to the creditors pro rata, gradually paying off the debt

affidavit
a statement in writing containing a person's evidence, on oath or affirmation. The evidence in the affidavit need not be expressed in any formal way but should be set out in numbered paragraphs. If the person making the affidavit wishes to refer to any document, this document can be attached ('exhibited') to the affidavit.

ancillary relief
general term for the financial or property adjustment orders that the court can be asked to make 'ancillary' to a petition for divorce or judicial separation

answer
the defence to a divorce petition, denying the allegations in the petition, or cross-petitioning

application
a document giving details, in broad terms, of the order sought from the court. All applications within divorce proceedings are started by filing a notice of application. Standard forms are available at divorce court offices; they include a space for the place, date and time of the hearing of the application, to be completed by the court office.

beneficial interest
the right of a person whether or not having legal ownership of a property to use or occupy it and to have a share in the proceeds if it is sold

Calderbank letter
where a husband knows he will be ordered to make payment if case goes to hearing, his solicitor writes letter making an offer of lump sum; if wife rejects offer and at hearing is awarded less, wife risks having to pay husband's costs incurred after date of offer

care and control
the responsibility for looking after and making everyday decisions about a child

in chambers
when the judge or registrar considers an application in private rather than in open court; the proceedings tend to be less formal than normal court hearings

charge
the security on property subject to which the owner holds that property, entitling the holder of the charge to be paid out of the proceeds of sale

child of the family
any child of both the parties and any child who has at any time been treated by both the parties as if a child of their own (but not foster-children); has to be listed in the petition irrespective of age

clean break
a 'once for all' order that deals with all financial issues between spouses and is not capable of subsequent variation even if circumstances change

common fund
costs payable to solicitor by legal aid fund

conciliation
a process intended to help the parties to reach agreement on issues concerning custody, access and related financial questions

co-respondent
the person with whom the respondent is alleged to have committed adultery

counsel
barrister

cross-petition
when the respondent puts forward in the answer different reasons for
the breakdown of the marriage from the petitioner's, and seeks a divorce
on those facts

custody
the right granted by a court order for one parent (or both) to make
major decisions for a child, such as education and upbringing, change
of religion, consent to marry

decree absolute
the order dissolving the marriage

decree nisi
document issued once the court is satisfied that the grounds for divorce
are established, allowing the petitioner to apply to have the decree
made absolute after a further six weeks if by that time the court has
certified its satisfaction with the arrangements for relevant children

directions for trial
the stage of divorce proceedings when the registrar considers the petition
and affidavit in support, with a view to giving his certificate for a decree
nisi to be pronounced by the judge

discovery
procedure by which each party supplies to the other a list of documents
relevant to an application and permits the other to inspect them

divorce court
any county court designated by the Lord Chancellor as a court where
divorce proceedings can be heard; also the divorce registry in London

domicile
legal concept, not necessarily related to residence: domicile of origin is
normally determined by the place where a person was born and is
retained unless a new domicile – a domicile of choice – is adopted by
a conscious decision to take up permanent residence in, and actually
moving to, another country

endowment mortgage
where a life insurance policy is charged to the building society or other
mortgagee as collateral security, the borrower pays the premiums to
the insurance company and interest only to the building society; if the

borrower dies or when the policy matures at the end of the mortgage term, it provides at least the amount needed to pay off the loan in full

equity (of a house)
the right to all or a share of the proceeds of sale (the net value after mortgage debts are discharged and expenses of sale met)

exhibit
document referred to in, sworn with, and attached to an affidavit

family assets
term used to describe property (including the matrimonial home and other capital items) acquired by husband or wife or both, in the anticipation that it would be used for the benefit of the family as a whole during their joint lives

filing
leaving documents – petition and accompanying documents, affidavits, notices of application – with the court office for sealing, and subsequent service

green form
popular term for scheme under which a limited amount of legal advice and assistance is given free or against assessed contribution

injunction
order by the court telling someone what he or she must or must not do; the penalty for disobedience can be imprisonment

legal aid
government-funded scheme administered by the Law Society based on financial eligibility and merits of case. What you pay towards your solicitor's bill is
—any contribution you are assessed to pay out of your disposable income and/or capital
—payment out of any money or property gained or preserved which is subject to the statutory charge.
Your being legally aided does not preclude your opponent being ordered to pay some or all of your costs. If costs are awarded against you, you personally have to pay (the legal aid fund will not) but your liability for your opponent's solicitor's bill will be limited to what the court finds reasonable for you to pay.

liable relative proceedings
proceedings taken against person legally responsible for maintaining wife or husband and/or children who has failed to do so

mortgagee
the building society, bank or other corporate lender or individual lending money on the security of a house or flat

mortgagor
the person who borrows money on mortgage usually to enable him or her to buy a house

nominal order
when recipient is entitled to maintenance but at the time of the order payment cannot be made or is not needed, an order for a nominal amount of maintenance (for example, 5p a year) is made so that if circumstances change, there is an order on the court's file which can be reviewed and varied

notice of application
form on which applications to the court are made, beginning with the words 'Take notice that . . .' and containing full details of what is applied for

party-and-party costs
the proportion of the other party's solicitor's bill which has to be met by someone who is ordered to pay costs

petitioner
the person who initiates divorce proceedings by filing the petition

postal divorce
colloquial term for divorce by special procedure

prayer
formal request in the petition, or answer, for the court orders which the petitioner or respondent seeks: for example, dissolution of the marriage, custody, costs, ancillary relief

registrar
judicial officer appointed by the Lord Chancellor; responsible for dealing with most of the applications to a divorce court

relevant child
child of the family under 16 years of age at the date of the decree or between 16 and 18 years of age receiving instruction at an educational establishment or undergoing training for a trade, profession or vocation (or up to any age, if disabled), in respect of whom the court has to express satisfaction before a decree nisi is made absolute

reply
document filed by the petitioner in response to an answer and/or a cross-petition from the respondent, containing the petitioner's defence

respondent
the spouse who is not the petitioner

sealing by the court
the court's stamping of a document when it is filed at the court office or of an order or decree when it is issued

secured provision
when some income-producing asset of the payer is put under the control of trustees and, if necessary, the income diverted to the payee to provide the maintenance ordered

service
the method by which the petition, notices of application, orders and decrees are supplied to the parties concerned; certain documents need to be served personally, others are served through the post, some by or on behalf of the person issuing them and some by the court

small maintenance payments
when a maintenance order is for weekly or monthly payments of not more than £33 a week or £143 a month to a spouse or to a child, or to a spouse for a child of not more than £18 a week or £78 a month, the payments are made in full without deduction of tax by the payer

solicitor-and-own-client costs
what solicitor charges his client (full cost of the case)

special procedure
in an undefended divorce, the decree can be issued without either petitioner or respondent having to appear (or be represented) at the court: the facts submitted by the petitioner in the petition and verified

on affidavit are considered by the registrar at the divorce court without either party being present. When he is satisfied that the facts in the petition are proved and that the ground for a divorce exists, he issues a certificate to that effect and fixes a date for the formal pronouncement of the decree nisi by the judge. A copy of the decree is sent through the post to both husband and wife by the court office.

statutory charge
the amount payable by legally aided person out of any property or cash that was in issue in the proceedings and was gained or preserved, where contributions to legal aid fund not sufficient to meet cost of the case (in matrimonial proceedings, £2,500 of gain is exempt)

summons
demand issued by a court for a person against whom a claim or complaint has been made to appear at the court at a specified time

Index

and legal aid 47, 49 *et seq*
value of 40, 47, 124, 125, 139, 141, 171
property adjustment order 20, 68, 69, 75, 120,
150, 158, 164, 173
applying for 122, 123, 124, 127, 138, 139 *et seq*,
176

rates 9, 46, 69, 83, 90, 172, 203
and housing benefit 64, 65, 183, 191, 200
reconciliation 17, 26, 27
registered title 79, 83, 124, 139
registrar 13, 122, 128, gl.
and financial applications 61, 99, 120, 122 *et
seq*, 127 *et seq*
and children 100, 101
and consent orders 73, 74
at county court 59, 153, 173
and divorce procedure 13 *et seq*, 23, 25, 26, 28,
210 *et seq*
giving directions 24, 125
information for 83 *et seq*, 91, 125, 126
and taxation of costs 153, 158
see also divorce court
registration
of court order 129, 165, 170
of land charge/notice 42, 78 *et seq*, 83, 139, 175,
205
of property 78, 79, 83, 124, 139
rent 46, 206
to ex-spouse 134, 137
and housing benefit 64, 65, 183, 200
resources 82 *et seq*, 92, 132, 197
calculating 87 *et seq*
disclosing 63, 65, 73, 74
respondent 13, 15 *et seq*, 22, 23, 25, 26, 120, gl.
acknowledgment of service 22, 24, 26, 120, 210,
211
answer 23, 120, 159, 211
applying for decree absolute 28, 213
and children 22, 30 *et seq*
and costs 159
and financial applications 59, 61, 96, 120 *et seq*
retirement 86, 89, 96, 165, 167

sale of home 68, 78, 79, 130, 133 *et seq*, 144 *et seq*,
166, 188, 193, 197
and CGT 136, 144 *et seq*
postponed 51, 55, 137, 181
Scotland 12, 148 *et seq*, 168
secured payments 67, 75, 120, 167, gl.
self-employed 84, 89, 108, 123, 124
and maintenance arrears 171, 172
Self-help guide for debtors 202
separation 10, 11, 22, 96, 120
affidavit on 25, 26
before divorce 12, 16, 17, 25, 75
and child benefit 66
and consent 22, 23, 120
judicial 13, 26, 32, 42, 59
and tax 102, 104, 105
SHAC 65, 208
Shelter 208
small maintenance payments 119, gl.
to/for children 112, 115, 185
to spouse 110, 111, 112
solicitor 26, 27, 29, 37

consulting 8, 12, 13, 26, 33 *et seq*, 58, 82, 128,
139, 159, 173, 174, 178
and conveyancing 10, 139, 180, 193
cost of 34 *et seq*, 82, 153 *et seq*
and defended divorce 22, 23
fees 40, 41, 48, 49, 58, 70, 153 *et seq* 158
and financial arrangements 73, 74, 82, 121,
126
fixed-fee interviews 37, 174
and green form scheme 42 *et seq*, 76, 78, 139
helping respondent 22, 23, 42, 155
information for 82 *et seq*, 91, 178
and injunctions 76, 77
and legal aid scheme 26, 45 *et seq*, 70, 147
Solicitors Family Law Association 37, 38, 39
special procedure, divorce 13, 23, 25, 26, 35, 45,
73, 159, gl
chronological stages 210 *et seq*
statutory charge, legal aid 49 *et seq*, 57, 58, 70,
127, 134, gl.
examples of 52 *et seq*
exemption 51
postponement 51, 55, 137
summons, gl.
judgment 171 *et seq*, 176, 204
supplementary benefit 14, 44, 56, 62 *et seq*, 86,
175, 195
allowances for children 100
or court order 63, 64, 129, 184
entitlement to 36, 42, 62, 66, 70, 183, 184, 191,
200
and maintenance arrears 170, 172, 177, 199
single payments 63, 205

tax 104, 117
and children 103, 112 *et seq*
deducting from income 44, 46, 85, 93, 123
examples of 104 *et seq*, 183 *et seq*
and maintenance 36, 102 *et seq*, 119, 127, 183
et seq, 195
personal allowances 73, 102 *et seq*, 183 *et seq*
reclaiming overpaid 108, 109, 113, 115
relief on loan 134, 135, 136
and 'small maintenance' 110 *et seq*, 185
and voluntary agreements 72, 73, 74, 104, 107,
109, 110
taxation, of solicitor's bill 153 *et seq*
tenancy
council 64, 84, 130, 132
private 65, 84, 130, 131, 206
and right to occupy 76 *et seq*
transferring 68, 130, 131

valuables 47, 84, 85, 88
ownership of 141, 142
variation of order 70, 73, 75, 128, 129, 164 *et seq*,
177
voluntary payments 72 *et seq*, 126
and tax 72, 73, 74, 104, 107 *et seq*

warrant of execution 171, 177
welfare officer, court 23, 32, 212
widow(er), pension rights 36, 85, 95, 96
wills 168